• THE ELEMENT GUIDE •

STRESS

Your Questions Answered

Rochelle Simmons

ELEMENT
Shaftesbury, Dorset • Rockport, Massachusetts
Melbourne, Victoria

First published in Great Britain in 1997 by
Element Books Limited
Shaftesbury, Dorset SP7 8BP

Published in the USA in 1997 by
Element Books, Inc.
160 North Washington St, Boston, MA 02114

Published in Australia in 1997 by
Element Books
and distributed by Penguin Australia Ltd
487 Maroondah Highway, Ringwood, Victoria 3134

Cover design by Bridgewater Book Company
Page design by R. Lightfoot
Typeset by Footnote Graphics, Warminster, Wilts
Printed and bound in Great Britain by
Biddles Ltd, Guildford & Kings Lynn

British Library Cataloguing in Publication
data available
Library of Congress Cataloging in Publication
data available

ISBN 1–86204–182–2

Note from the Publisher

Deep relaxation could alter required medication in conditions such as diabetes. Any information given in any book in the *Element Guide* series is not intended to be taken as a replacement for medical advice. Any person with a condition requiring medical attention should consult a qualified medical practitioner or suitable therapist.

Contents

To Marianna

Her world is full of wonder as she sees it for the first time.
May it ever be thus.

To see a World in a Grain of Sand
And a Heaven in a Wild Flower,
Hold Infinity in the palm of your hand
And Eternity in an hour.

William Blake

Acknowledgements

With grateful thanks to Barry, Carlos, Kirsten and Naomi for their help and support and to all my students and clients who have taught me so much.

Introduction

The image often associated with stressful living is that of the top executive jetting around the world, attending a multitude of meetings and making rapid decisions. The truth is that stress presents difficulties to people in every walk of life: business or professional persons, the employed or self-employed, students, people involved in home and family. Stress can be the result of too much pressure, or boredom, or lack of direction. So this book is for the outwardly agitated, those who have bottled up their feelings, busy people, and those who are understimulated.

Research is now demonstrating the effects that stress can have on health. People who are living with high levels of unresolved tensions may be accumulating invisible chronic illness (ICI). It has been recognized that inappropriate reactions to extreme anger can put people at risk of developing coronary heart disease. Tension can be related to high blood pressure, can affect the immune system, the rate of healing and can cause lack of sleep and fatigue. People who are over-stressed often find that their relationships suffer and that their general levels of efficiency diminish.

There is a growing interest in understanding the techniques of coping with stress and courses are springing up in centres of adult education, helping more and more people to take active control over managing their stress levels. Many companies are beginning to realize that their staff members are more productive when they are able to deal creatively with stress and, as a result, courses are being arranged in the workplace.

The following pages can be used as guidance for such courses, although they have been written primarily for use by individuals or among family and friends. You might enjoy forming a group and setting aside a regular time to work through the suggested activities and discussion points that are presented in the boxes.

This book starts by helping you to recognize when stress is complicating your life. It then offers a two-pronged attack on how to deal with it: physical stress control, and stress management. The relaxation techniques will teach you to understand your physical reactions to stress. You will learn the general techniques of relaxation, then ways of applying these skills to deal with emotional and physical discomforts. If you want to focus mainly on these skills, you will find them explained in chapters 6, 7 and 8. (If you prefer not to learn physical relaxation, then these are the chapters to skip.)

The chapters dealing with stress management will give you a chance to look at yourself as a personality and at your lifestyle. You will work towards getting your life into a comfortable balance, and consider ways of dealing with overload and how to say 'no' without guilt. Here will be the opportunity to look at planning and coping mechanisms that can be tailor-made to your own life experiences.

My emphasis is on bringing fun back into our lives. Stressed people tend to take themselves very seriously and give themselves a bad time. By getting back our sense of humour and changing our perception, onerous tasks can become challenges and games, and we can reclaim the child in ourselves. We can start experiencing life as an adventure rather than a treadmill. We may not always be able to change what happens to us as we go on life's journey, but we may be able to change how we feel about it and how we react.

The human being is a beautifully designed machine that needs to be allowed to function well. When we are tense we clog up the works; we often look after our cars better than ourselves! So let us aim to understand what is going on in our lives. Once we have awareness, we can make choices, we can aim at becoming a smooth, purring engine, well-oiled and efficient. By taming the stress in our lives we can make it work for us, we can turn a harsh master into a good servant.

CHAPTER 1

What is Stress?

THE FUSE BOX

When people are over-stressed and full of tension they may desperately feel the need to do something about it but hardly know where to begin. They may grit their teeth and battle on, or may turn to inappropriate ways of dealing with the problem: the medicine chest, the drinks cabinet or the packet of cigarettes. Sometimes they get caught up in 'driven' behaviour: more work, frenetic 'work outs', spending sprees.

Often, they are slow to realize what is happening to them. If this applies to you, here are a few symptoms that might help you to recognize that you are pressurized:

- taking longer and longer to do a job
- increased memory lapses and accidents
- getting agitated and anxious easily or flying off the handle
- tiredness, sleep disruptions
- no personal time
- low morale

HOW DO WE DEFINE STRESS?

Whenever I ask people to define stress for me, I find that, mostly, they give examples rather than definitions. They talk about trying to juggle with too many tasks; about having too many demands made upon their time;

about trying to battle on while feeling ill or in pain; about trying to run the home while the builders are causing havoc.

What these examples have in common is that they all require us to adapt to the demands put upon us. So we are moving towards a definition. How about this one?

Stress is the body's response to any demand made upon it.

Yes, this is all right so far, but we need more. We have a built-in desire, both physically and emotionally, to be in a state of balance. In other words, we need to adjust in order to cope and to make ourselves more comfortable. So we have an increased demand for readjustment. Stress, then, also has something to do with adaptation in order to re-establish normality.

We can now extend the definition:

Stress is the adaptive response to any demand put upon a person. It requires adjustment to re-establish a normal balance.

STRESS OR DISTRESS?

The examples people give tend to be of an unpleasant nature. They are describing distress. But stressors (this is what we call the causes of stress) can be nice or nasty. Whether the stress is fun or a horror, it is still putting on pressure. The demands on the person and the need for adjustment remain the same and it is only the depth and the number of stressors that affect the ability to cope.

Pleasurable stress is exciting, so we tend not to recognize it easily. But if it is too much for us, we can still become pressurized. Distress is horrid, so we focus on it with anguish, feel sorry for ourselves, get angry and dis-contented; thus adding even more pain. Sometimes we give ourselves a bad time! What we need to remember is that, nice or nasty, stress is using up our physical and emotional resources.

There are four stages to our responses:

- the alarm reaction (the quick lift)
- temporary exhaustion (after a superficial demand)
- the coping stage (long term, which physically wears us out)
- complete exhaustion (no more coping resources)

The bank manager might describe it like this:

- Michael draws money out of his current account to settle an unexpected bill.
- He has a temporary cash flow problem.
- He regularly draws from his investments that have been stored away.
- He has nothing left and becomes bankrupt.

We have, in varying degrees, the ability to muster our energy and 'rise to the occasion'. The exhaustion after this temporary demand is superficial and, if we allow ourselves to recuperate, is reversible. Being in a constant state of alert, however, is a different matter. This draws from our deep stores of adaptive energy. These are reserves that can be depleted and can wear us out. Our adaptability is finite.

The choice is ours. We can squander our reserves of energy recklessly by 'burning the candle at both ends', or we can learn to make this valuable asset last longer by using it wisely and with care. We need to choose to cut down on the distress and making sure that we fill our lives with activities that are worthwhile and joyful.

ACTIVE AND PASSIVE DISTRESS

We tend to associate stress with busy, pressurized people, whether executive or housebound. They are experiencing active distress. Lack of adequate stimulation and fulfilment, however, can be a cause of passive distress, and we must, therefore, also address the needs of people who have lost motivation, are bored or are too tired to function joyfully.

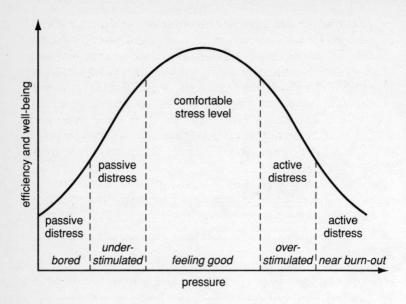

CAUSES OF STRESS AND STRAIN

Let us look at a number of different areas that can put us under pressure. We should be positive so perhaps I would do well to change the way I said that. Let us look at a number of challenging areas for which we need to be in a state of alert and that require us to use our adaptive skills.

Our reactions depend on:

*Depth of Stress and the Number of Stresses
at Any One Time.*

Loss

Loss throws us into a state of bereavement. I use the word bereavement here to refer to *any* loss. We all understand the pain we experience when we lose someone we love. This must, surely, be the greatest pain of all. We go through a process of disbelief, low self-esteem, lack of direction, lack of lustre. In varying degrees, we encounter a similar process in all situations where loss is experienced: the loss of a job, the loss of possessions, the loss of reputation. Even coming to the end of a project or particular personal achievement that has given meaning to your life can be stressful. Those of us who have worked for exams will remember that strange flat feeling once the exams are over and it is possible to sit down without an open book in front of us.

These are the times when we have to be extra kind to ourselves while we work out a new *raison d'être* and adapt to the new circumstances of our lives.

Have you had any losses in your life recently?
How has this affected you?
What adaptations have you had to make?

Boredom (passive distress)

We can feel stressed in any situation that we may perceive as lacking in stimulus. This may be hard to believe as we tend to think that only too much pressure is distressing, but an empty life can cause its own tensions. We shall be looking at this in much more detail in chapter 11.

Is your life feeling more empty at present than you would wish?

Performing tasks

Whenever we have a new task to learn, we are using up our adaptive energy. It gets easier with practice. I remember how I felt when I started to learn to drive. There was so much to concentrate on: what my hands were doing, what my feet were doing, trying to notice everything that was going on the other side of the windscreen, remembering the rules of the road . . . Then it became second nature. The tasks were the same but the stress was less. I had brain space to listen to the car radio, talk to my passengers or plan what I would be doing later that day. The task hadn't changed – only the way I responded to it.

When I taught school leavers, I had to use all my powers of persuasion to keep my young pupils from either despairing or actually walking out of their jobs during their first month of employment. They moaned to me that they were permanently exhausted, found it difficult to keep up with the level of concentration needed for the job and had no energy for a social life. I encouraged them to cut down on any activities that were not strictly essential. If they felt the need to come home and just flop into bed, they should do just that. 'Is this all there is to adult life?' they would wail. One month later, once they had adjusted, they painted a different picture. They started to discover that this is not all there is to adult life!

Are there any new tasks that are using up your energy at present?
How do you help yourself when you are in this situation?

Frustration

This is what we feel when we have no power over what is happening to us. Many of us prefer to take some control over our lives and when this is lost we experience the distress of being victims. For many of us, this is the hardest stress of all to bear. We cannot change what is happening to us, only how we feel about it and how we react to it. This change is quite a challenge.

I once knew an elderly lady, Mrs Peterson, who would sit silently and listen attentively, while everyone around her spoke. From time to time she would come out with the only sentence that I ever heard her utter. She would nod her head knowingly and say, 'Well, that's how it is!' Then she'd shut up again. I could never work out whether she was very stupid or very wise. But I do quote her often so I assume she must have been very wise.

Whenever I come up against a frustration that makes me want to scream, I nod my head, just like Mrs Peterson, and say 'Well, that's how it is!' There is some value in accepting that which cannot be changed. We save a lot of energy which would be wasted on yelling, kicking, fighting against it, or feeling sorry for ourselves.

Do you focus on the frustrations in your life?
How much energy do you waste banging your head against a brick wall?
Make a list of situations where you might make a Mrs Peterson response.

Danger

We feel stressed in any situation that we *perceive* as threatening. I emphasize the word 'perceive' because our reactions are very much a personal response. For example:

1 Gerald is going on his first trip abroad. Aeroplane travel is a new experience for him and he knows little about it. The plane starts to shake and rumble. His heart starts to beat faster, he breaks out in a sweat and feels very frightened.

2 Andrew, sitting across the gangway, works as air crew and is taking a well-earned holiday. Being airborne is second nature to him and he notes briefly that they are experiencing some turbulence before continuing to read his newspaper.

The same situation has evoked two different responses: same situation, different perception.

We do not respond universally even in situations that might be seen objectively as dangerous. One person's danger might be another's adventure. Some people imagine threat round every corner; some see the world as a dangerous place and are in a permanent state of alert.

Do you see life as a battle?
How do you respond to threats and what can you do to make yourself feel safer?

Physical Stress

If we are coping with pain, illness or disability, we are permanently under stress from within. As we have only a finite capacity to adapt to pressure, we start at a disadvantage with limited reserves. It often takes very little to bring us to toleration level. People who get used to constant physical stress sometimes forget how much they are coping with and are surprised and guilty when they feel they cannot take any additional load. Others may be thoughtless and can impose on those who are already carrying a burden. We have to take care that we do not make martyrs of ourselves.

External physical stresses can also take their toll: living in constant danger can be draining; pollution stresses both body and spirit. To what is normally termed as pollution I would add extremes of temperature and noise.

I once visited a school which had an unaccountable reputation for behaviour problems and frequent staff turnover. It was situated very near to Heathrow Airport. When a plane passed overhead the noise level in the classroom was intolerable. Each time the noise increased and then decreased the teacher raised and then lowered his voice so that he was changing pitch every two minutes in order to be heard. As he raised his voice, I saw the children tensing visibly. So there were two-minute cycles when the teacher spoke loudly and the children tensed, then spoke softly and they calmed down again. I most certainly didn't consider the problems of the school unaccountable. By the time I returned home that evening, I felt drained and knew I would never wish to spend another day in that environment.

> Are there any internal physical stresses that you have to endure?
> Are there any environmental stresses that you frequently experience?
> Have you considered how you can ensure that you do not exceed your tolerance level?

Lifestyle Changes

Although we may be really happy about some of these changes in our lives, they do require a lot of adaptation from us and, as a result, they are stressful. Here are some lifestyle stressors that you may or may not welcome.

- marriage
- new baby
- new home
- new job
- divorce
- redundancy
- retirement
- family parties (eg Christmas)
- holidays
- changes in: responsibility at work
  working hours or conditions
  sleeping habits
  eating habits

> How many lifestyle changes have you experienced this year?
> What adaptations did you have to make?
> Are you satisfied with the way you coped or could you have made it easier for yourself?

If we don't want the fuse box to blow, we have to make certain that we can cope, both physically and emotionally, with the load that the circuit is carrying. We all know the saying 'It's the last straw that breaks the camel's back' and I have to admit that it is usually the small, unimportant extra pressure that makes me lose my cool after having coped magnificently with the tough problems.

Let me remind you – it is the depth and number of stresses at any one time that makes us blow a fuse. We have a responsibility to ourselves to phase our activities so that we do not overload. Chapter 11 gives a practical guide on how to deal with this problem.

CHAPTER 2

The Nature of Stress

A STATE OF ALERT

How well do you know your body? Under every sophisticated and thoroughly modern person there is a primitive body – a caveman or woman, physically speaking. Let us imagine what type of lifestyle you, the primitive person would have experienced. Let yourself go back in time. You are living in a cave using your own instinctive responses in order to protect yourself and your nearest and dearest. From what do you need to protect yourself? What skills do you require to be thoroughly efficient in this task? Let us picture you face-to-face with a sabre-toothed tiger. What do you need to do? You have two options: you can fight, if you are able or, if you are more like me, you can run away. For both you must have maximum muscle strength. Your body needs to switch into fight or flight mode. A number of things are likely to happen to enable your body to cope when confronted with a dangerous or difficult situation. These are the healthy fight or flight responses:

- Your heartbeat and pulse may increase.
- Your blood pressure may go up.
- Blood will pass to the large muscles in the body.
- *Your breathing becomes faster.*
- *You breathe using the upper part of your thorax – so you may pant.*
- Your mouth may go dry.
- You may feel sick.

- You may feel the need to empty your bowels or bladder.
- *Your muscles may tense up.*
- Perhaps you will sweat, especially your palms.
- You may have indigestion (acidity).
- The hairs on your skin may stand on end and you could shiver or get 'goose flesh'.
- Sugars and fats will probably be released into your blood for quick conversion into energy.

All these reactions take place as extra oxygen is carried by your blood, from your lungs to the large muscles in your body. In your muscles, carbohydrates are burned up in order to release lots of energy. This is the energy you need for flight or fight. Remember this is the healthy and successful way of responding to a stressful reaction. The primitive body is at its most efficient to deal with the stress. Only body functions that are absolutely necessary take place, others shut down temporarily.

But when did you last come face-to-face with a sabre-toothed tiger? Well, yes, you do regularly – but in a different form.

- You are in your car, late for an important appointment. The tailback goes on for miles. You try to detour. So do dozens of others. You are caught up in an even worse jam. Now you will be even more delayed.
- You return from the supermarket, laden with bags, step into the kitchen – the washing machine has flooded!
- You settle in front of the TV for a well earned half-hour. The telephone rings. It is your elderly mother phoning for the sixth time. Now she wants you to come round to change a fuse.
- You are walking towards an important meeting. You want to look good. A car passes too close and too fast, drives through a puddle and spatters you in mud.

The trouble is that these modern tigers cannot be killed with brute force. So the primitive body perceives the 'danger' and responds in the only way it knows; it prepares you to use your reserves of energy to fight the beast – but the beast cannot be beaten in the primitive way.

Make a list of your most commonly encountered tigers.
Then look at the fight or flight response list above. You would not be aware of some of the reactions mentioned because they are going on inside you, but there are others that you could easily recognize.
Tick those that you know you experience.

The body meets a stressor (modern tiger). It responds in the primitive way with energy made available for the big effort – but the problem cannot be solved in a physical way. The body is now in a state of alert but to no avail.

Not all stresses are of a physical nature. Some people become so used to battling their way through life, that they see the world as a dangerous place. Being tense and in a permanent state of alert becomes normal behaviour. They are not just faced with anxiety-provoking situations but find it impossible to unwind even if they cannot identify the tigers.

Being alert in this way we call being in a state of arousal.

HOW DOES BEING IN A STATE OF AROUSAL AFFECT US?

Now is the time to start watching other people. We can learn a lot from observing others.
Can you think of people you know who often seem very agitated?
Can you recognize when they are in a state of arousal?
Notice how they are sitting or standing; what are their hands doing, what are their facial expressions?
Listen to their tone of voice, their speed of talking, whether they are always 'looking on the black side'.
Write down or tell a partner what you observe.

Now, here is a question to ask yourself. What does it feel like to be with tense people? Do you find yourself mirroring their behaviour?

When I was a teacher I spent some time watching young, inexperienced colleagues in action. When they attempted to control an unruly class, they demonstrated many of the characteristics listed above; as they became more distressed, the general excitability of the class increased. As their voices became louder and shriller, the noise in the classroom rose to compete. These classes were not comfortable places to be in. Now, I wonder if my early years in teaching were so exhausting because I, too, may have erred in the same way. The 'old hands', and hopefully I became one, would meet noise and excitability with calm, quiet voices, speaking slowly and using lower vocal registers. As a result the children calmed down without even realizing it. In other words, even if they wanted to throttle the little devils, they were not going to let on that they were ruffled. Moreover, I can tell you that a lot more work was done. Try it out for yourself, it really gets results.

Now think of people you know who appear calm. Make a list of the characteristics they demonstrate. Notice what it feels like to be in their company. Do they make you feel good?

So what are *we* doing to people around us? Are we good to be with or are we spreading tension and distress? It feels great if people seek us out because we are a haven of contentment and are fun to be with.

HOW TENSION AFFECTS OUR ABILITY TO FUNCTION WELL

Let us look at what tension does to our efficiency.

> The young bull and the old bull stood on a hillside looking down at a herd of cows.
> 'Let's charge down the hill,' said the young bull, 'and mount a few cows.'

'No, sonny,' said the old bull. 'Let's saunter down the hill and mount *all* the cows.'

Have you noticed how, when you are in a hurry and anxious, you make more mistakes and get less done? Can you remember what you have or haven't done? Did you really turn off the gas? Did you lock the door?

> Face a partner, linking both hands with your partner
> *or*
> hold onto a door handle that can be pulled very hard.
> *Now, pull as hard as you can, making a great effort.*
> *While you are pulling, say the names of all your relations in age order.*

How well could you concentrate while making a physical effort? Not too well, I guess! So it looks as if muscle tensions and strain make our thought processes less efficient.

Most of us are familiar with the 'tip of the tongue' experience. We try to remember a name, it's right there, in our minds, but it refuses to be recalled. As soon as we relax, stop trying to remember, or are just about to fall asleep – then the memory returns.

Being in an unnecessary state of arousal is very uncomfortable. It uses up our energy but is unproductive. If we are tense and over-anxious, we make our own lives a misery and are not pleasant to be with. In fact, allowing the caveman to control the civilized person just gets one on a downward spiral of inappropriate and self-destructive behaviour.

Life is fun! So let's make the most of it!

The world is not full of obstacles, but full of challenges, a series of adventures. We cannot always change what happens to us but we do have the power to change the way we feel about it and the way we behave.

Tigers can be tamed!

The rest of the book will show you how.

CHAPTER 3

How Well Do You Know Yourself?

ARE YOU YOUR BEST FRIEND OR YOUR WORST ENEMY?

Competition is instilled in us at an early age. We try to live up to its demands and values in our attempt to achieve social acceptability and success. We grow up being assessed and graded at school. Our schools are assessed and graded nationally. At work we try to keep an inch in front of our peers. Material possessions (or the wealth to buy them) are status symbols. We are constantly looking over our shoulders. For recreation, many of us indulge in competitive games or sport either personally or vicariously, supporting a team or an admired player.

It is not my intention to try to turn this ethos on its head. After all, positive stress is the motivation that makes us function effectively and creatively. But we can easily become anxious about our performance. We might start questioning if we are good enough. The need to succeed, and our intolerance of failure, can compound the strain that is on us. Tense people are not efficient. They very quickly lose concentration, easily get tired, start chasing themselves round in circles, mislay things. This quickly moves to loss of self-esteem and possibly panic. In short, life becomes very uncomfortable – and the effect can be contagious!

HOW STRESSED DO YOU FEEL?

Ask yourself these questions from time to time to check your progress.

1 **I get sudden panic feelings**
   not at all ☐
   only occasionally ☐
   quite often ☐
   very often ☐

2 **I feel anxious and wound up**
   most of the time ☐
   frequently ☐
   from time to time ☐
   not at all ☐

3 **I have a strange sensation as if something awful is going to happen**
   not at all ☐
   not very much ☐
   quite often ☐
   a lot of the time ☐

4 **I keep focusing on worrying thoughts**
   most of the time ☐
   frequently ☐
   occasionally ☐
   not a problem ☐

5 **I get agitated feelings like butterflies in my stomach**
   not at all ☐
   sometimes ☐
   quite often ☐
   very often ☐

6 **I can sit still and feel relaxed**
   not at all ☐
   not often ☐
   most of the time ☐
   always ☐

7 **I feel restless and have to keep active**
   very often ☐
   quite a lot ☐
   not very much ☐
   never ☐

Stress rating score

Questions 2, 4, 6, 7
   box 1: 3 points
   box 2: 2 points
   box 3: 1 point
   box 4: 0 points

Questions 1, 3, 5
   box 1: 0 points
   box 2: 1 point
   box 3: 2 points
   box 4: 3 points

How stressed are you?

16–21 You are probably very uncomfortable indeed and would certainly benefit from trying to change. !!!

9–15 There is quite a lot of tension in your life. You would do well to work on it.!!

2–8 You have a moderate level of tension that could certainly be improved.!

0–1 Either you have it exactly right or you are not recognizing your tensions. If you have been attracted to this book, the chances are that you feel that you might enjoy focusing on some stress-related topics. We learn and change all the time!

WHAT ARE THE OPTIONS?

When we come up against a brick wall, we have a number of options. We can:

- stand and bang our heads against it
- exhaust ourselves trying, but failing, to climb over it
- 'blank out' and stand and stare
- turn away from it immediately and go back
- step back, assess the problems, plan a strategy and possibly decide to make a detour

> Can you remember a time when you were definitely not coping well?
> Which of these options did you take?
> Did you respond in a way that was useful and creative?
> Did you get caught in a pattern of behaviour that caused you yet more distress?

HOW DO *YOU* REACT?

It is valuable to build up a profile of any aspects of your behaviour that would indicate to you that all is not well. We express our distress in a number of ways:

- body tensions
- physical behaviour
- interpersonal relationships
- mood and thought processes

Apart from our thoughts, these can easily be recognized by others. Often we are the last to realize that we are in trouble. Perhaps we could use the people close to us as a resource. If we are not offended by their comments, we can accept them as helpful support. We can ask questions like, 'What do you see me doing that tells you that I'm tense?' Remember, we want observations, not solutions or directives.

Body tensions

As our bodies are primitive, they often express our distress before we are truly aware of it. Think of people you know well. Can you tell what mood they are in even from behind? Can you understand their body language in the way they sit, stand, move around? What about facial expression? Do they frown, stare, tighten their mouths?

Do you recognize what *you* do?
Are there any discrepancies in your behaviour? Do you smile while discussing difficult topics, or say 'everything's fine' while tensing up your muscles? Check it out with your friends.

Sometimes body language can be symbolic of something that is causing us anxiety. Several examples have entered into common parlance, 'He squared his shoulders and battled on'; 'She is carrying the troubles of the world on her back'; 'Just grin and bear it!'; 'We grit our teeth with determination.'

Physical behaviour

Do you recognize when your coping patterns cause more problems than they solve? Do you rush around at great speed, getting nowhere? Do you become clumsy, dropping and breaking things? Do your movements become jerky and inaccurate? Do you lose things, forget facts, lose concentration? Do you go blank or day-dream? Do you find yourself doing extra, unimportant tasks – doodling, faffing around, going off at a tangent?

Remember a specific day when you were aware of being strained. Which coping patterns did you apply that you know were doing you no good at all?

Interpersonal relationships

People who are reaching burn-out can be very unpleasant companions or colleagues. They often find it hard to give us their complete attention; they get agitated when trying to communicate with us. They have a tendency either to blame others for what is going wrong, or to be self-deprecating, blame themselves and appear to be self-absorbed; they can be snappy and tetchy and generally spread discomfort around.

Can you recognize when you are doing any of these things?
Can you think of any occasion when you allowed your tensions to foul up contact with another person?

Mood and thought processes

Some people experience mood swings, flying from bursts of frenetic activity to lethargy. Their thoughts can be gloomy and pessimistic. Some feel they just want to run away from it all, or they feel incompetent and experience low self-esteem. Some are aware of a sense of being 'got at'.

Do you recognize any of this?
What goes through your mind when you are feeling tense?
Are your thoughts useful or do they encourage your bad feelings?

Look over your list of personal reactions to strain. You can see that they do not help to solve any problems. In fact they compound the pressure by expending energy – energy that you cannot afford to waste. You want to learn to use this precious gift of energy in a way that is not self-destructive but self-enhancing.

Now that you have learned how to take stock of your reactions and have built up a 'tension profile', you are in a strong position. You know how to identify signals which tell you all is not well. You can acknowledge to yourself that you are distressed. Only now can you try to take action. As you become more skilful at recognizing your own personal signals, you will find that you start to notice them earlier, before they become overwhelming. It is far easier to unravel a simple knot than one which is a complete tangle.

HOW MUCH DO YOU NEED?

Sandy and Susan are friends of mine. Sandy is a caring mother and wife. In addition she is a high-powered business woman, manages a large staff, jets around the world for international meetings and enjoys her leisure pursuits of tennis and squash. Susan lives alone. She enjoys staying at home with her books and television and is genuinely content not to go out. She once suggested that I postpone visiting her as she had a busy day ahead: she had to get up half an hour earlier to pay the milkman! Both my friends appear to be truly contented with their lives, although their lifestyles could not be further apart. What they have in common is that they each acknowledge the level of stress that they enjoy and make certain that

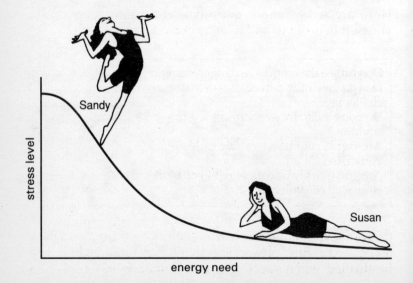

they get it. They are functioning at their Comfortable Stress Level.

There is no universal right or wrong, only right or wrong for you. Some of you will thrive on creative stress. If you are experiencing more stress than you need, or too much of the wrong type – pressures that cause strain rather than excitement – then you suffer from *active distress*. If you have a high need but are under-stimulated, then you are experiencing *passive distress*.

Are you a high-energy or low-energy person?
Where do you come on the Sandy–Susan activity scale?
Mark in your Comfortable Functioning Level.
Where would you place your current situation on the Sandy–Susan scale?
Are you currently above or below your Comfortable Functioning Level?
Are you experiencing any active or passive distress? (*See* graph in chapter 1.)

Here are a few more questions you might like to ask yourself in order to add to your personal profile.

Do you see the world as a dangerous place, full of obstacles?
Do you generally perceive tasks as onerous or as exciting challenges?
Do you tend to focus on the difficulties or the advantages of a situation?
Are you at your best working to deadlines or do they cause you distress?
Are you quickly impatient with yourself or others?
How well can you tolerate failure?

Of course excitement and stimulation need not always be associated with physical activity. A birdwatcher will be thrilled when spotting a rare visitor to his garden. A correctly completed crossword puzzle can bring great satisfaction. A painter or handicraft enthusiast may never venture far from the armchair. So include your level of need for mental or creative stimulation in your assessment.

You have now built up your unique profile that can help you to honour your needs. Remember that you have certain rights:

- the right to be truly yourself and not to have to emulate others;
- the right to be comfortably at the level of stress that is suitable for you;
- the right to change if you wish.

CHAPTER 4

Body and Mind

SETTING THE SCENE

A SENSE OF WELL-BEING

It isn't just in the mind! Feeling good actually improves health. The 'Achilles heel' conditions – irritable bowel, rashes, backache, migraine – although not necessarily caused by tension, get worse when people are under strain. It is thought that tension has a debilitating effect on the immune system, predisposing people to colds and other disease, and that being in a state of alert physically inhibits tissue repair. Healing takes place when the body is at rest.

It also seems that laughing and having a good time actually have the physical effect of toning up the body, and laughter is a great releaser of tension.

> Some years ago, my husband, unhappily, had to undergo daily radiotherapy. Our son visited us and gave us a video of the complete series of one of our favourite comedies with a prescription stating 'Take two daily for four days.' We still remember the healing light of our laughter shining out of those dark days.

What is your Achilles heel? Do you see it as an extra burden or a sign that you must start taking more care of yourself?
What makes you enjoy a really hearty laugh? How can you ensure that there is a lot of fun in your life?

HEALTH AWARENESS

Persistent poor health and lack of fitness are internal stresses that can take their toll of your resources. Perhaps you are unfortunate enough to be suffering from some chronic sickness or pain and there is nothing to be done about it. This means that you have fewer reserves to deal with extra tensions and are likely to reach burn-out quicker than those who are fit. It is important to be honest with yourself, to face up to the facts, and take stock of how you are disadvantaged. You deserve to care for yourself so think about how much extra pressure you can realistically take before you reach saturation point. You are probably far more protective of your nearest and dearest than you are of yourself. It might be useful to ask yourself, 'What would I advise another if they were in my situation?'

Imagine that someone in your situation is sitting in the opposite chair. Be a good friend and help to plan a strategy for keeping extra pressure away.

Regular exercise strengthens the muscles, heart and lungs but is also a useful releaser of tension. Try slowly to increase your physical activity: walk instead of using transport, take the stairs rather than the elevator. Indulge in any activity that you know you really enjoy: swimming, aerobics, sport, dancing.

Draw up a plan to gradually increase your physical fitness. Decide whether you can proceed alone or whether you need the support and camaraderie of other people.

Eat healthy meals. Stress often worsens people's eating habits. They might snatch a quick snack or compulsively tuck in to comfort foods. This can lead to a poor supply of the vitamins, minerals and fibre that the body needs to have in order to work at its best. Feeling off-colour or putting on weight can all add to the original stress, producing a vicious circle. Emotions related to eating are complex. It is sometimes revealing to explore the significance of food in your life and family, now and in your past. You might consider if it has been a medium for reward or punishment or if the dinner table has been the family's traditional 'battleground'. We each have the right to break with any personal attitude or family tradition that makes us uncomfortable. We have the right to change.

> How will you make a commitment to improve your eating habits and make meal-times a source of health and pleasure?

Tobacco and excessive use of alcohol or caffeine (in coffee and tea) act as temporary props. Their effect is short term, they can let you down with a thud and leave you having to come back for more. Caffeine is a recognized stimulant, well known for producing insomnia in many people which can also lead to some people feeling unusually jumpy and nervous. These reactions are already problems associated with high levels of stress.

CALM THE SENSES

The five senses are taste, sight, hearing, touch and smell. Senses are the way the body receives messages about the environment which can affect mood. Individuals respond differently so they should know which senses are important to them. By recognizing personal sensory responses people can add to their pleasures in life and can set the scene to enhance a relaxing ambience. The *oral* person responds to food as a source of pleasure. A 'foodie' doesn't just eat to live. The *visual* person easily makes mental pictures – pictures of memories, pictures of how something might look in the future, can easily imagine scenes, is affected by scenery, room layout and colour. The *aural* person can easily repeat what has been heard, remembers music, responds to sounds and is aware of pleasant or unpleasant tones, volume and pitch. The *tactile* person remembers sensations of touch, responds to textures and shapes and is calmed by stroking or massage. The *olfactory* person reacts to the stimulus of scent, finds smells can trigger memories, can be easily offended or easily pleased by aroma. Most of us are a good mixture of all of these but we tend to find some senses more important or more acute than others.

> Which of the senses are most important to you?
> What do you do to ensure that you set the scene to help yourself to be relaxed?

Oral people need to cultivate a positive approach to eating. Food can be a great delight as well as being health-giving. Meal-times should be healthful and pleasurable experiences. Food should be attractively prepared and presented. It is wise to prepare well-balanced meals, with plenty of fresh fruit and vegetables, low in saturated fats, and including unrefined, vitamin-rich and fibre-rich versions of bread and cereals. Meals should be at set-aside times and places and deserve your full attention. Try to sit down in a relaxed place kept especially for eating rather than snacking at your desk, or standing up, or while doing other tasks. If it is possible, protect yourself from the tyranny of the telephone. You know yourself best and will decide whether you prefer eating in company or alone, or with music, soft lighting, while listening to the radio or reading. It is up to you to make your meal-time one of the highlights of the day. Allow yourself to fully savour the food; eat slowly, enjoying the appearance, smell and full flavour of it. Give yourself special treats. There is little that is actually harmful if enjoyed in moderation. For example there are only 60k calories in a piece of chocolate. If you love chocolate as much as I do you would find it a punishment to do without altogether. So hold your chocolate, enjoy its appearance and aroma. When you put it in your mouth let it linger. Move it around your mouth with your tongue and chew it slowly, letting yourself appreciate the full flavour. Afterwards let your tongue pick up any remaining taste in your mouth and on your lips. Hopefully, after allowing yourself such sensual pleasure, you will feel satisfied and will not need to wolf down the rest of the box.

Visual people need to make certain that they are calmed by the scenes and colours around them. I love the countryside and remember regularly making a detour, on my way to a very stressful job, in order to pass green fields. The effect on my mood well compensated for the extra time spent. A friend of mine was unwell and housebound for many months. Her distress was significantly lightened by the fact that she could sit in her reclining chair and watch the activity of the birds and the beauty of her much loved garden. Some colours are stimulating and others calming. A visual woman I worked with told me that just the thought of the colour blue was enough to get her started when practising relaxation. When doing close work it is relaxing to change focus and look into the distance from time to time. Pictures that feature avenues of trees leading towards the horizon have a calming effect (and might be usefully placed opposite a dreaded dentist's chair).

Aural people need to be aware of what type of music calms them. They might like the sound of wind chimes or bird song. For some, singing or playing an instrument can be a great stress releaser but, if they are anything like me, preferably without an audience. There are two types of helpful relaxation tapes, those that talk you through a relaxation script and those that just produce calming sounds. Recently I found myself in two different hospital departments that could have been anxiety provoking. The staff in both were aware of the therapeutic value of music but in the first department I was greeted by raucous pop music; all right for many, no doubt, but not for me – it just added to the discomfort! I had no intention of being a martyr and asked for it to be turned off. In the second department, before being enclosed in a scanning tunnel, I was asked for my musical preference. I spent a restful 20 minutes entombed with my beloved Schubert. We must be careful to ensure that we are not making assumptions about the taste of others, and we have a right to see that no one makes assumptions about *our* needs.

Tactile people should be aware of the fact that they are sensitive to comfortable furniture and might consider treating themselves to a reclining chair, a good supporting upright armchair, or a tip-up relaxer; they often like using footstools. They might find that a warm bath is a good way to start a relaxing evening. Temperature is very important to them and they may enjoy changing into comfortable clothes. Remembering childhood comfort, some like holding fluffy toys or handling pets. Perhaps they benefit from doing knitting or embroidery. I've noticed that when my mother knits, a great aura of calm emanates from her.

Olfactory people need to surround themselves with the smell of fresh air, a favourite perfume, scented candles and flowers. They can enjoy the fragrance of coffee, wine and food as much as the taste. They are more likely than others to use aromatherapy products.

Aromatherapy, however, is much more than just the sensation of enjoying pleasant smells; there are a number of ways that essential oils can be used which can affect mood, and it has long been known that plant products can have powerful effects on the body. Aromatherapy works on the principle that the body absorbs substances not only by mouth, but through the skin, lungs and the membranes lining the nose. Essential oils can be purchased from specialist shops and some chemists. They can be used either for relaxation or stimulation in a number of ways. For *massage*, the oils are diluted in a vegetable base oil. Specialist shops sell it already mixed but you can add the drops to your own choice of cream or gel. If you are a tactile person and have a willing companion, some simple neck, shoulder and back massage can really help you unwind.

Alternatively, you could use a body oil on yourself The use of *compresses* is a good alternative to massage. Put a few drops of the essential oil into warm water. Dip a small towel, or bandage, into it and wring it out, then place it over the areas where muscles are in need of extra help to relax. You may choose to place it on your forehead, the back of your neck or across your shoulders. You might enjoy adding drops of your favourite fragrance to your *bath*. Generally, exhilarating oils are used in the mornings and relaxing oils are used at night. I have found that a few drops of lavender oil on my pillow when I go to bed works wonders. The use of *oil burners* is a lovely way to set the scene in a room; they are available commercially and make good gifts for others or for yourself. A small cup is placed on top of the burner and filled with water to which are added a few drops of the oil of your choice. A lighted calorette or warming candle is placed underneath. The aroma subtly diffuses throughout the room. There is a wide range of oils on the market for you to experiment with. Here are a few suggestions to get you started.

For relaxation:lavender, clary sage, geranium, camomile. For exhilaration or refreshment: thyme, rosemary, basil, any citrus.

THE BODY IN BALANCE

The skeleton gives rigidity to the body. Muscles are attached to the bones and by contracting and relaxing enable movement to take place. Muscles are situated in antagonistic pairs, so that when one muscle contracts its partner relaxes and vice versa. In this way the body stays in balance, which aids circulation and the removal of waste products.

Hold your arm out straight and notice how your triceps at the back shorten and tense while your biceps in the front become longer and relaxed.
Pull your wrists to your shoulders and feel your biceps bulge and tense as your triceps become longer.

Whether the body is moving or still there is always a combination of muscle tension and relaxation. If a good balance is not achieved, the body suffers excessive muscle tension which can cause pain, strain and fatigue. If muscles are held tightly in static contraction, circulation is impeded and this results in a build-up of fatigue products. These cause cramp-like spasms. Tense people are more likely to have aches and pains, especially in the neck and shoulders. Just holding the fist clenched for a while can raise blood pressure.

If you want to stand without strain, hold your head comfortably on your neck, drop your shoulders and keep your weight on the balls of your feet. Be aware of any mannerisms that unbalance you such as bending one knee and putting more weight on one foot, or raising one shoulder and holding your head to one side. When you walk, swing from your hips, keep your movements easy and comfortable with no stiffness. It is useful to notice how you hold yourself in photographs or ask people whose judgment you trust.

1 Hold a piece of hair from the crown of your head. Pull it up gently and imagine that it is a plumb-line passing down through your body.
2 Imagine that you are a puppet with strings across your shoulders and up to your head. Say to yourself 'up and sideways', and feel the pull as your neck stretches and your shoulders drop and stretch out, slightly downwards. Can you feel the pull between your shoulder blades?

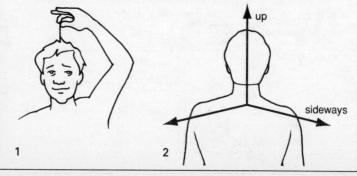

1

2

Do you sit low in your chair with your legs sprawled out?
Do you keep your legs crossed, your hands clenched or your
shoulders hunched? Try sitting well back enjoying the
support of your chair, with your feet slightly apart and flat on
the floor and your hands gently open on the arms of the chair
or in your lap.

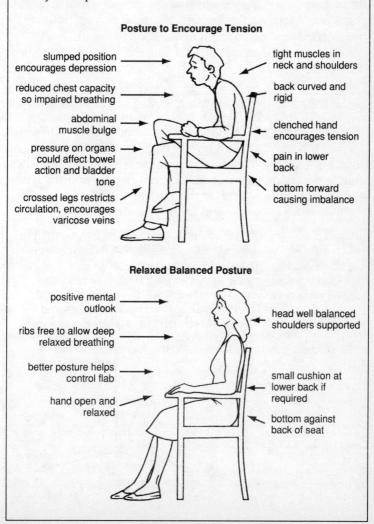

Posture to Encourage Tension

slumped position
encourages depression

reduced chest capacity
so impaired breathing

abdominal
muscle bulge

pressure on organs
could affect bowel
action and bladder
tone

crossed legs restricts
circulation, encourages
varicose veins

tight muscles in
neck and shoulders

back curved and
rigid

clenched hand
encourages tension

pain in lower
back

bottom forward
causing imbalance

Relaxed Balanced Posture

positive mental
outlook

ribs free to allow deep
relaxed breathing

better posture helps
control flab

hand open and
relaxed

head well balanced
shoulders supported

small cushion at
lower back if
required

bottom against
back of seat

If you also want to protect your body from pain, strain and fatigue, when bending, lifting or pushing, the balance theory must again be applied. The general principle is to bend at the knees, keeping the plumb-line operating when reaching down. If necessary, kneel or sit on the floor. When lifting an object, get down to it and lift it to a halfway stage before standing and lifting it the rest of the way. Push from the shoulder or back rather than with outstretched arms.

The body in balance is a beautiful working model. Keep it that way!

POSTURE – THE MESSAGES WE GIVE OURSELVES AND OTHERS

Social psychology teaches us about the enormous impact of what is called non-verbal communication, generally known as body language. As it is so important we need to be fully aware how we use this form of expression.

A game to play with others

Write on separate pieces of paper various of scenarios that express different moods. For example:

> Your number has come up on the lottery.
> Your job application has been rejected.
> A close friend is seriously ill.
> You have been invited to stay in the country.

Try to find examples that range over as many different emotions as possible.
Select a paper and try to convey the appropriate emotion physically and without sound. Let the others guess the mood and then let them suggest possible themes.

How often have you asked 'What's wrong?' of someone as they walk into a room? Do you instantly feel trusting if you deal with people who appear calm and efficient? The body language of others has a powerful effect on us. Your body language is your 'hot line' to the outside world but also confirms what you feel about yourself. Here are a few observations that you might recognize. No doubt you will be able to add a few of your own.

Tense/aggressive

taut, rigid stance	squared shoulders
hands on hips	clenched fists
standing too close	eyeball to eyeball contact
arms folded (body closed off)	sarcastic smile

Anxious/lacking in confidence

shoulders slumped	inappropriate smiling
looking away	playing with hair
fidgeting	wringing hands

Calm/comfortably assertive

comfortable eye contact	shoulders relaxed
hand gestures (for emphasis)	appropriate distance
body still and calm	arms unfolded

Usually you express physically what you are feeling, but if you are not happy with the messages you convey, this can be turned on its head to your advantage. You can defy the anxiety; just *act* as if you are calm. If you consciously change your behaviour, you will generally find that you start to feel differently about yourself, and others may start to respond differently to you.

Stand in front of a long mirror.
Try out some of the body language listed above.
Notice how you look and how you feel when giving tense or anxious signals.
Change to a calm, comfortable expression and notice how your appearance and feelings alter.

AFFECTING MOOD WITH THE VOICE

When you speak, the tone, pitch and tempo of your voice communicate a great deal more than just words.

Look back at the body language expression game.
Play it again but this time instead of using just body language to express feelings, add non-verbal vocal sounds.

We can now add some vocal clues to our list.

Tense/aggressive

sarcastic, sneering tone	loud voice
deathly soft voice	firm, clipped speech

Anxious/lacking in confidence

soft voice, hard to hear	whining voice
shrill tone	very fast speech
trailing off at end of sentence	hesitance
nervous cough	over-use of er, um etc.

Calm/comfortably assertive

appropriately warm and/or firm	slower speech
use of lower registers	comfortable pauses

Once you start to convey a calmer demeanour, you will be amazed at how quickly it can become your normal way of behaving. It will not only affect the way you feel but will have a knock-on effect on others. You will be a pleasant person to be with, and you will certainly find it easier to think clearly.

The next chapter takes a deeper look at body language and how you can use it to understand yourself more fully.

CHAPTER 5

The Internal Conversation

HOW OFTEN DO YOU TALK TO YOURSELF?

How often, when you have a problem, have you been advised to talk it over with a good friend? But what is a good friend? Is it someone who listens, one who tells you what to do, one who commiserates and re-enforces the bad feelings you may already have, or someone who helps you to analyse and evaluate your situation? Is it fair to give this responsibility to friends and can they ever measure up? If they are not skilful as counsellors, are they no longer good friends?

   In this chapter I suggest that your best bet is to become your own friend and ally. So my advice to you is talk it over with *yourself*. It is really quite difficult to talk creatively to yourself, to develop the art of *inspeak*, but for your own stress management, it is an art worth learning.

WHAT IS THE INTERNAL CONVERSATION?

If you remember, a strong source of distress is frustration, which I defined as not having control over what is happening to you. In order to regain that power over your own life it is necessary to be assertive. Assertiveness is being able to honour your own needs without disregarding the needs of others. It is about taking action instead of reacting to situations that have been set up by others.

   The internal conversation consists of talking to oneself through five key questions and answers:

1 What am I feeling? What am I doing?
2 What emotions am I expressing?
3 What is this telling me?
4 What do I want?
5 What can I do about it?

Very often the first four questions remain unanswered as people leap into responses that may not be in their best interest. They are being reactive, but were they able to employ inspeak they would free themselves of the pressures of being victims of circumstances.

Some people deal with pent-up feelings by having a good scream, crying, bashing a cushion, digging up potatoes or taking a brisk walk. If this describes you, and neither you nor others are hurt by these actions, it is no bad thing because at least it releases tensions. There is, however, a big BUT – don't leave it at that! If nothing changes as a result of frustration, you may well end up caught in a circle of *accumulating tension – dramatic release – same again*. For your greater comfort you need rather more self-knowledge than that. If you fall into the trap of just saying 'that was bad' without analysing why, you are taking no action to prevent a recurrence. Likewise, if you say to yourself 'that was good', without acknowledging why it was good, you may end up having no part in giving yourself satisfying experiences. In both cases you will be subject to the whims of fate.

Once you are aware of mounting tension, this is the time to act decisively. The first thing to do is STOP! Then, STAND BACK! After that your internal conversation can begin.

Inspeak can be carried on inside your head or by speaking aloud. At the risk of appearing to be slightly dippy, I must admit that I find speaking to myself aloud is the most successful way I know of really getting my thoughts straight. I do, of course, have to choose my time and place and only occasionally find myself muttering away while walking in the street. Try it for yourself.

Choose a phrase that has some meaning for you.
It could be something like 'I am not afraid.'
Try saying it inside your head.
Now say it aloud and repeat it a few times.
Does it feel different to you?

YOUR INTERNAL IMP

Everyone has an internal imp. It is that inner saboteur that tries to wreck our clear thinking and action. It is that little nagging voice that tells us that our judgement is faulty, that we have failure built in to whatever we do, that we can never be good enough. Every time Imp gets the upper hand it jumps up and down gleefully and yells 'I told you so, you're rubbish!' It will probably rear its ugly head at each stage of your internal conversation. It may represent what you think you *ought* to do rather than what you *want* to do. It may represent your fear of failure: the part of you that has yet to find the courage to take risks, the part of you that does not trust yourself to be competent or at least good enough.

Try to visualize your own personal imp – perhaps it is an animal or a fanciful creature.
What are the early signs which indicate your imp is playing up?
How can you quash it? (Find the funniest methods you can think of – tape up its mouth, lock it in a trunk, put a sack over its head.) Don't try to kill it – it is, after all, part of yourself.

PLAY FOR TIME

It can be very stressful when people want you to make decisions quickly, but it isn't necessary to jump into action whenever others require it. You have a right to take your time if you need to consider what you really want. Perhaps you can get through your internal conversation very quickly or you may need to take yourself away and carefully consider your position. You may risk being labelled slow witted. You don't have to accept that judgement and might find yourself rephrasing that accusation, 'No, I'm not slow witted, but I do need time to work out how I feel about that.' You are likely to employ your own ways of helping yourself to take thinking time and here are a few extra phrases that you might choose to adapt to your own need:

I'll phone you back on that one.
I'd like to think about that.
Hmm . . . well, let me see . . .
So let's go over what we're saying here . . .
So, what you're saying is . . .
Let's see if I've got that right . . .
I'm not sure what I want; I need some time on that one.

THE FIVE KEY QUESTIONS

1 What am I feeling? What am I doing?

You have probably learned early in your life to be 'well behaved' and to shut down on your emotions. (We all do this to some extent but the degree varies from person to person.) Your body is less civilized and probably recognizes and expresses your feelings even when you are not conscious of them. Your body talks in code; it talks to you using *body language* which involves positions, movements, muscle tensions and changes in breathing.

In the previous chapter I suggested you learn to recognize these messages in order to deal, as early as possible, with the build-up of pressure. You may now wish to add to that skill by learning to crack the body code in order to read that language more fully. Remember that as body tensions are the way your body communicates with you,

you could welcome them as they are going to lead you to understand yourself more completely.

So, stage one of your *inspeak* will start with:

STOP!	STEP BACK!
Are my muscles tight?	How am I breathing?
What is my posture doing?	How am I moving?

Do you have an Achilles' heel, some physical discomfort which you recognize is triggered by stress? This could be tension headaches, migraine, bowel irritation, painful shoulders or stomach discomfort. Acknowledging this discomfort could also be the beginning of breaking your code. If your symptoms actually make you ill, it might be worth looking at what being sick allows you to do. Are you now justified in saying 'no' (sorry, I'm too ill to do it) or taking time for yourself (I must go to bed, I'm ill), or expecting care for yourself (please look after me, I'm ill). If this is what you, the sick person, needs, then this is what the sick you must have. But in addition, it may be worth trying to satisfy those needs at times when you are not ill, so that you become free to say 'no', to take time for yourself and to expect care without the punishment of sickness. Can you get what you want without being a martyr?

Recognize discrepancies

Does your body ever give you (and those you communicate with) conflicting messages? Is there a disagreement between the meaning of your words and your tone of voice, or between what you are saying and how you are acting? Here are a few examples that I have observed:

1 Dorothy: 'I'm fine, thank you.'
   Me: 'You say you're fine, but your voice sounds flat and you are gripping your chair.'
   Dorothy: 'Well actually . . .' Followed by what is really bothering her.

2 Guy says at an interview that he has no problem with a particular task. His body says otherwise; his hands are tightly clenched, he frowns. Which is telling the truth, his words or his body language?
3 Alison frequently makes hurtful comments with a smile. Is she expressing her own confusion or is she trying to confuse me?

You might try out saying one thing and expressing another as an exercise in order to start recognizing the discomfort. Eventually, you may come to sense this discomfort whenever you find yourself doing it 'for real'. Then you can allow the alarm bell to ring, give yourself time to stop, and try to work out what you are doing.

2 What emotions am I expressing?

Once you have recognized body tensions, your next stage is to understand what emotions they may be trying to express. You have five emotions: joy, contentment, fear, anger and sadness. Very often you may be experiencing a combination of these and they may be telling you about a collection of feelings you are experiencing. For each of these emotions there will be a range of intensity. Here are a few of the reactions you might experience, you could find extra words of your own:

Joy: glad, gay, excited, mirthful, exultant, rapturous.
Contentment: calm, peaceful, pleased, quietly happy, satisfied.
Fear: worried, apprehensive, anxious, scared, frightened, in a panic, terrified.
Anger: fed up, put out, annoyed, resentful, angry, raging.
Sadness: upset, unhappy, distressed, bereft, distraught.

You may find it difficult to know what you are truly feeling. Perhaps you think that understanding your emotions is self-indulgent, or you may have learned at an early age, either at home or school, that you should swallow your feelings and battle on. If you have ever observed young babies, you could not fail to see that they express emotions in extreme form without any reserve. There is nothing as pure as a baby's rage. You had no problem in experiencing emotions when you were newly born but, as you became trained to become socially acceptable, you learned to shut down on them. The difficulty arises when this control goes too far and you become distanced from your feelings. Now is the time to try to reach those hidden expressions with the maturity that protects you from becoming a screaming child again.

You are at the stage of your internal conversation when you are asking yourself, 'What are my body tensions telling me about how I feel?' If you are aware of resistance to acknowledging these feelings you may need to break yourself in gently at first and then allow yourself to test the stronger feelings. For example: 'I'm a bit fed up . . . Well, really I'm rather annoyed . . . Actually, I'm very angry!'

You may find it useful to talk yourself through an *emotions scan*. This is a 'feelings check list' that could help you to seek out which emotions you are expressing.

You could ask yourself –
   Am I feeling sad?   Am I feeling frightened?
   Am I feeling angry?
Then you could state aloud to yourself –
   I am feeling sad!   I am feeling frightened!
   I am feeling angry!

Some people find their emotions become more easily accessible if they bash a pillow, say any words that come into their head, or take themselves to a quiet place to contemplate. You will know how you can best access your own feelings.

Just recognizing your feelings and experiencing them may be all you want for a while. You can only move on when you are ready and in your own good time. Do be cautious, however, if you find yourself getting stuck with an emotion that causes you pain. You may decide that you want to risk taking small steps forward (and possibly back again) to test the water. You may need to risk the hurt and ask yourself if you can survive it.

3 What is the emotion telling me?

Let us look at what our five emotions express.

Joy: I am excited.
Contentment: I am satisfied.
Fear: I am afraid of something (a shared reality or perceived).
Anger: My needs are not being met.
Sadness: I have lost something (concrete or perceived).

We can now explore more fully what this means to us:

Joy: What excitement am I enjoying at the moment or what excitement am I anticipating?
Contentment: What has satisfied me or what is at the moment giving me satisfaction.
Fear: What am I afraid of or what am I risking?
Anger: Which of my needs are not being met? What do I want which is different from how things are at present?
Sadness: What have I lost or am about to lose?

Many of our experiences engender a variety of emotions and often they appear to be conflicting ones. For example, an adventure can cause anxiety and yet excitement. Anger can lead to action which results in satisfaction, and is often confused with blame and aggression. It is not necessary to be angry *with* someone or *with* oneself, although what a person does can make us angry. Attributing blame could be a waste of useful energy which may not lead to solving the problem. If the focus is on recognizing the need, the next stage of the conversation becomes attainable.

4 What do I want?

Do you feel guilty about considering what you want? What you want isn't necessarily being selfish. You might find that there is a conflict of needs and that it is important to you to be a good parent/child/sibling/employer/ employee. In this respect, you may decide that your need to support another is more important at the moment than your need to promote yourself. You may decide that you wish to be non-assertive and take no action. You can choose to do any of these things, but it is a considered thought if it takes place at this stage of the internal conversation. You are asserting the right to behave as you wish and you can take responsibility for your action or non-action. After all, life need not be a battle that you have to win.

You might get some clues about your needs by making objective statements about yourself:

I am quiet . . . I need a calm, peaceful atmosphere.
I think and act slowly . . . I need time.
I am orderly . . . I need an uncluttered space.
I respond well when I am urged on . . . I need encouragement.

If you need some further help in becoming aware of what you truly want, you might find it useful to use one of the following aids:

1 Write your ideas down in a 'thought diary' (random thoughts and ideas as they occur to you).
2 Speak your thoughts into a recorder.
3 Let yourself get deeply relaxed and then imagine yourself making a request of your fairy godmother. Start every sentence with the words 'I need'.
4 Make a list of words that best describe what you are feeling, then see where they lead you.
5 Project the existing situation on to a screen. Then change the details until you feel that the outcome is the best you can achieve.

Sometimes, trying to give further definition to the words you have used to describe how you are feeling might help to give you insight into what you want. For example, using the word 'resentment' could mean that you are caught up in a commitment that you don't want to be in. The word 'frustration' might indicate that you are in a situation over which you have no control. If you are 'fed up' you may feel that you can take so much but enough is enough.

If you want to get an overview of what is happening, try to describe the situation from your own point of view and then through the eyes of others. If you speak or write in the first person, imagining you are that person, you will find it easier to understand how others are thinking and feeling. This might help you to move into the fifth stage.

5 What can I do about it?

Now that you have awareness, you have a choice of how you respond. If you are experiencing an emotion that indicates you are in distress you will probably be in need of consolation. So an attempt should be made to give yourself some comfort. It is so easy to slip into the habit of being a harsh self-critic and you probably find it much easier to comfort others. Perhaps you might imagine how someone else could be kind to you, then decide not to wait for them, but support yourself instead.

This is the time to look at a list of your personal criteria for measuring success. Sometimes the ability to tolerate 'failure' may paradoxically be a 'success'.

You may find that your answer to question five is simply 'accept it'. You may not always be able to change what is happening to you but at least your perception could change. An onerous task, for example, could become a challenge. If you are experiencing fear of some type, once you have acknowledged it, you could decide to go ahead just the same – to feel the anxiety and get on with it anyway. If you remember that fear is the other side of excitement, once it is accepted, it need not grind you to a halt. As anger is the emotion that can get you in touch with your needs, it is also the source of energy for change. We are not talking about attack and blame, but the driving force that is behind motivation which leads, eventually, to the joy and contentment of achievement.

Chapter 11 looks at the way forward and offers suggestions that might help.

A sample internal conversation

Q1 What am I feeling and doing?

A My shoulder muscles are tensing, I'm clenching my fists. I have just made a sarcastic comment.

Q2 What emotion am I expressing?

A I don't really know.

Q Are you feeling angry . . . frightened . . . sad . . . ?

A Yes, I think I am annoyed and a bit anxious. Yes, I'm angry and frightened.

Q3 What is this telling me?

A I don't want to compete for this contract. I'm afraid I shall not measure up at the meeting.

Q4 What do I want?

A I want to accept that I may lose it. I want to realize that I can only do my best and it is possible that I might fail. I need the confidence to know that even if I do this badly, there is much that I do that is good.

Q5 What can I do about it?

A I must prepare myself thoroughly for the meeting, using any help available. I must face the fear and find the courage to risk failing. I might need to think of alternative pathways as a support. If unsuccessful, I will take care to be self-supporting and not blame myself or others for the outcome.

CHAPTER 6

Introduction to Relaxation Techniques

GET TO KNOW YOUR MUSCLES

WHY LEARN RELAXATION?

You are about to start practising a technique that helps you take responsibility for your stress reactions. Through learning the luxury of letting go you will set out on a journey of self-enhancement. You will travel on a route towards achieving the pleasure of a tranquil mind in a calm body: an overall feeling of well-being.

Physical relaxation may appear easy, but it is a skill that has to be learned and practised. When we watch toddlers trying to get around, they may at first crawl, totter, take a few steps and then run back to mother for safety. Eventually they will be able not only to walk and run with grace, but to negotiate hazards and choose directions. By this time they will be able to journey without having to focus on the expertise needed. That is the joy of practising skills; eventually they become second nature and we no longer have to concentrate on them. But for now, we must start our journey as toddlers. Our destination is a lifestyle that could be serene, calm and creative.

In the chapters that follow you will learn the general skills of relaxation and then ways of applying the techniques to deal with emotional and physical discomforts so that you will be able to be at ease with yourself and others in all sorts of situations.

These are some of the emotional and relationship areas where people have found that applying relaxation techniques have helped:

insomnia	agitation	anxiety
lack of confidence	tense situations	dealing with others

I am not suggesting that relaxation is a cure-all, but it is possible to reduce greatly the distress of many physical conditions. Here are some of the problems that have been relieved:

migraine	nervous headaches	indigestion
high blood pressure	tight muscles	backache
irritable bowel	chronic pain	post-operative healing

I must emphasize that you should not diagnose yourself if you are suffering any physical symptoms. You should always seek a medical opinion. However, learning to relax in order to cope with discomfort can do no harm and has no side effects. In fact, relaxing deeply actively helps recovery and repair. If your condition is found not to have any organic cause and is a direct response to tension, then perhaps relaxation alone may solve your problem.

HOW RELAXATION WORKS

Look back at the fight and flight responses in chapter 2 (pages 11–12). Three reactions have been highlighted. These, relating to breathing and muscle tensions, are the only ones over which you have any direct control. You can learn to slow down your breathing, to breathe deeply and to relax your muscles. Amazingly, as this starts to happen, so the other responses change automatically. For example, if you calm your breathing and relax your muscles you will find that your pulse will slow down, shaking will stop, nausea will go away and the palms of your hands will become dry.

The relaxation training will guide you through a series of

carefully graded exercises and games that will give you back control of your breathing and muscle tensions, and help you to calm your mind.

RECOGNIZE MUSCLE TENSION AND RELAXATION

The habit of tensing muscles has a way of creeping up on us. It becomes our normal way of behaving and it is often only when we are extremely muscle bound, perhaps suffering from bad backache or neckache that we finally realize what we are doing. Tight muscles have to scream at us before we notice them. You don't want your muscles to control you; you're the boss! So you have to train yourself to notice what tension feels like in all the muscle groups in your body before you can attempt to relax them. A good way to do this is to go steadily through the body, first tensing and then relaxing each set of muscles.

If you want to make your own recording to listen to, you could read the following script for a tense/relax exercise onto a cassette recorder. Leave plenty of gaps in your reading as you don't want to rush yourself. You can then lie back and follow the instructions easily. Don't worry about how well you perform. You will get better as you practise. So just enjoy the experience. The word RELAX is repeated frequently. This is not because I have mislaid my thesaurus, but because some people find it valuable to associate letting go of tension with a key word. You might prefer to choose a different one for yourself.

Get into a very comfortable position. You may either sit or lie down. Close your eyes, relax your arms and leave your legs uncrossed. Let yourself feel heavy and limp. Think of the word RELAX as a focus while you are letting all tension flow away from you. Let a feeling of warm relaxation take over as you let go more and more. Don't try to control your breathing. Follow your own natural rhythm. Let your breathing be regular, gentle and relaxed. Breathe in and out through your nose. As you breathe in, feel your abdomen rise slightly. As you breathe out, say the word RELAX to yourself as you feel yourself sinking.

As you tense and relax the sets of muscles in your body, you will learn to recognize the difference between tension and relaxation in your muscles.

First focus on the muscles in your legs and feet. Tense these muscles by straightening your legs and pointing your toes down as if you were trying to make your legs 10cms longer. Keep stretching and feel the tightness in your calves and ankles – and RELAX. Let the muscles become loose and soft.

Now concentrate on the muscles in your thighs, hips and lower back. You can tense these by pressing the tops of your thighs and buttocks together. (If you are a woman – pull up your pelvic floor muscles between your legs at the same time.) Imagine that you need to visit the toilet but have to wait. Relax the muscles in your buttocks and thighs and let your legs fall apart feeling heavy and limp.

Now focus on the muscles in your abdomen. Pull them in tightly. Imagine you are wearing a very tight belt – and let go. As you feel the relaxation spread across your abdominal muscles notice the difference between tension and relaxation in them.

Think now about the muscles in your chest. If you take a big breath you will tense these muscles. Now breathe in as big a breath as you can and hold it. Feel as if you are wearing a sweater that is two sizes too small. Feel the tension in your chest – and slowly let the breath out. Now return to keeping your breathing regular and gentle. Each time you breathe out, say the word RELAX in your mind and let yourself unwind more and more.

And now tense the muscles in your shoulders. Make a big shrug and draw your shoulders up to your ears as tightly as you can. Hold it – and RELAX. Drop your shoulders. Feel the tension ease away. Focus on the word RELAX as you breathe out with loose and comfortable shoulders.

Next, focus on your triceps. These are at the back of your upper arms. With palms upwards, straighten your arms as hard as you can. Push back and feel your arms tensing. Imagine you are trying to flatten your arms back against a wall or flat onto the floor. Concentrate on the tension – and RELAX. Let the muscles at the back of your arms feel completely relaxed.

Now think about your biceps. These are in front of your upper arms. Tense these muscles by bending your arms at the elbows. Pull your wrists towards your shoulders but keep your hands relaxed. Feel your biceps tensing – and RELAX. Let your arms fall back.

Tighten the muscles in your hands and forearms. Clench your fists as tightly as you can to tense them. Clench tightly. Imagine the sensation you would have if you were using a screwdriver on a very stubborn screw. Feel the tension – and RELAX. Relax and remember what it felt like to have tension in your hands and arms and notice how different they feel now that they are comfortably relaxed.

Now focus on the muscles in your neck. Press your head back as hard as you can and feel the tension in your neck. Hold it – and RELAX. Now your head can balance gently. Enjoy the sensation of tightness passing away.

There are many muscles in your face. I want you to learn to recognize what they feel like when they are tense and when they are relaxed.

Firstly, tense the muscles in your forehead. You can tighten these by raising your eyebrows as if you were very surprised. Feel the tension. Hold it – and RELAX. Let your eyebrows drop. Let your brow go smooth.

Tense the muscles round your eyes. Frown as hard as you can. Pull tightly. Squeeze hard – and RELAX. Let your eyelids stay lightly closed. Concentrate on the word RELAX and remember the different feelings between tension and relaxation in the muscles of your forehead and around your eyes.

Next tense up the muscles round your mouth. Press your lips together as tightly as you can and purse them as in a very exaggerated kiss. Press tightly – and RELAX. Let your lips rest lightly together, soft and comfortable.

Focus on the muscles in your jaw. Bite your teeth together as tightly as you can. Feel the tension – and RELAX. Part your teeth slightly and leave them comfortably apart.

Now concentrate on tensing the muscles of your tongue and throat. Put the tip of your tongue up against the roof of your mouth and push as hard as you can. Imagine you are trying to swallow a large pill. Feel the tightness in your tongue and throat. Press up harder – and RELAX. Let your tongue rest softly at the bottom of your mouth behind your bottom teeth.

Let that feeling of warm relaxation flow from your toes to your head and down again, let it wash over you. Remember what it felt like to have tension in your muscles and notice how it feels now, to be relaxed, comfortable, calm and serene. Stay relaxed for a few moments enjoying the sensation of tension released. Then take a deep breath, stretch and bring your practice session to an end.

Many people have told me that after doing this *tense/relax* exercise they have become aware of muscles that they didn't know they possessed. So now they are able to recognize when they are tightening them! That is why it is so important to repeat the exercise above. This is a way of introducing you to your muscles so that you can be more intimately aware of your own reactions. How frequently you practise and for how long you continue is entirely up to you. Some people find that a daily practice session is useful until they feel confident that they are truly sensitive to their responses, which might take anything from a few days to a few weeks.

I must emphasize that the *tense/relax* exercise is a training to help you feel the difference between tension and relaxation in your muscles. This is not the final relaxation experience. Once you can easily recognize the sensation of muscle tension you need no longer ignore it. You will then be ready to move onwards to learn *Deep Relaxation* (chapter 8) which enables you to totally unwind your whole body without any tensing up.

TENSION RELEASE TRIGGERS

As you become more and more aware of your muscle tensions in your practice sessions, you can start to apply that consciousness to other times of the day.

> Can you notice how your muscles tense when needed to do a normal task?
> Do you easily relax your muscles after the task is over?
> Do you tense up extra muscles that are not needed for the task?
> Do you tense your muscles when they are not needed at all?
> Are your muscles tensing to express your feelings rather than being used as 'tools'.

Your muscles are very valuable tools. You should exercise and strengthen them but be master over them, not a victim to their whims. Start to pay attention to your particular ways of tensing up. On the diagram opposite shade in the areas that you know you habitually tighten. Perhaps someone who knows you well might have some comments to make too.

As you become aware of your tight areas you can start trying consciously to relax them. If you find it difficult at first, you might prefer to exaggerate the tension as in the *tense/release* practice in order to be aware of the difference. As you improve you will be able to let go after only the very beginning of tensing.

These personal areas of muscle tension can be used as your *tension release triggers*. As you allow yourself to focus on them they will tell you that you are not relaxed. My chief triggers are the muscles in my shoulders. As I sit at my desk

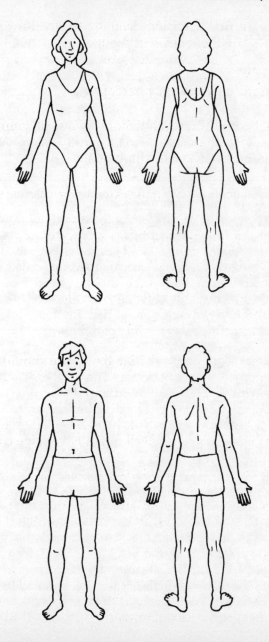

I am aware that my shoulders start moving up and up. Once I release the tension in these muscles, the rest of me follows suit. You may find it useful to check your triggers at regular intervals and then deal with them. If your triggers are more diffuse you may need to start regularly using a check list or body scan.

| What is my brow doing? | What are my shoulders doing? |
| What are my hands doing? | What is my jaw doing? |

Do you have any mannerisms that might tell you that you are unnecessarily tensing your muscles? Some common ones are doodling, fidgeting, gripping the arms of your chair or the steering wheel and gnashing your teeth.

Once, when I was wearing open sandals, a friend commented that I had 'very mobile toes'. Now I have added toes to my check list as I have noticed that, often, when I think my muscles are at rest, my feet, hidden from view, are dancing away for no good reason!

I remember sitting an examination in a very large hall where I had to work hard not to be disturbed by the jittery behaviour of the other students. Around me I could hear the rustle of sweet papers, the scraping of chairs and at the next desk, a man who spent the best part of three hours tapping his pen on the table. I had to be resolute in my effort to devote my attention to the task in hand. It would have been easy to blame others for my inattentiveness. Instead, it was necessary to confirm to myself that these people were demonstrating some inappropriate responses to the stressful situation we were in. It was their problem not mine.

A woman in my stress class reported back that she could not practise relaxation that week because there were road works outside and the noise was too intrusive. She was blaming others for her inability to relax and had to go away with a new determination to welcome the opportunity to put her newly acquired techniques to the test. She eventually learned to accept the challenge and remain calm even when those around her were running riot. She found that by understanding that the noise had nothing to do with her, she could take responsibility for her own reactions.

- Acknowledge the annoyance.
- Don't blame.
- Recognize that it has nothing to do with you.
- Get back to the job in hand.

RECOGNIZING THE BEGINNINGS OF TENSION

When your unnecessary muscle tensions have become very strong and habitual, you will find it is very hard to master them. That is why it is important not to wait until you are completely muscle-bound. If you can pick up the very early stages of your tensing, you will be able to deal with the situation quickly and effectively.

Tighten the muscles in your shoulders very slightly so that you can feel them pulling even though you have not moved them noticeably. Relax.
Lay your hand palm downwards on a table, pull your fingers back to tighten your muscles slightly, see if you can feel the tension without actually seeing any movement. Relax.

AIDS TO SUCCESS

Some people find that they can assist their progress when learning a new skill by keeping a diary. Here they can record any difficulties they may encounter and how they overcome them. It is helpful to list new achievements and for some, a grade on a scale of one to ten can be useful. If you have a tendency to put yourself down or are easily discouraged, be careful, make sure that you are constructive in your criticism and use encouraging words.

Please don't worry about your progress. No one will be assessing you. Very few people have a 'Eureka!' moment. Change takes place slowly, gets easier with time and is completely personal. Your use of this book may be very different from someone else's and there are no rights and wrongs. The book is here to guide and help you – to hold your hand as you go on your journey. But it is your responsibility to make it a good experience for yourself.

CHAPTER 7

Take Responsibility for Your Breathing

SIGH AWAY THE TENSION

Breathing is such a fundamental part of life, the first and last act, that it has become a metaphor for life-force. The word is used in many ways to describe reactions that might have emotional overtones in phrases such as:

catch one's breath (with delight or fear),

with bated breath (restrained by reverence or fear)

breathe down someone's neck (over-supervise)

stop for a breath (take rest or refreshment)

breathtaking beauty

waste one's breath (talk to no avail)

You may remember that in the list of fight and flight reactions to being in a state of arousal, chapter 2, three responses were controllable and two of those were related to breathing.

There are four stages to breathing:

1 Breathe in
2 Breath held in
3 Breath out
4 Lungs empty

Sit quietly and pay attention to your breathing.
Recognize the four stages but don't try to control them.
Try to notice what each stage feels like.

Did you notice that stage 1 and 2 are the tensing parts of the cycle and that 3 and 4 are the relaxing parts? On inhaling, the muscles between the ribs, the abdominal muscles and the diaphragm (that sheet of muscle cutting across the body under the lungs) all tighten in order to make the chest cavity larger. This causes air to pass into the lungs. While breath is held, all these muscles remain tensed. When they relax, the ribs, which have been pulled up and out, drop back to their original position, the abdominal muscles, which had bulged out, flatten, and the diaphragm which is flat when tense, returns to its relaxed dome-shaped position. When empty, the chest remains in the relaxed position. So the muscles used to breathe are constantly tensing and relaxing. Comfortable, healthy breathing, therefore, brings the air down into the depths of the lungs and the body is able to relax as the breath is let out. When in a state of arousal, breathing becomes faster and the muscles in the upper part of the chest take over to cause panting. This is very useful if a lot of energy is being used up for physical effort and fighting tigers! At other times it can cause hyperventilation (over-breathing) which can result in dizziness and can compound feelings of agitation.

Have you observed people breathing in a tense way, with shoulders hunched, the upper part of their chests heaving and air taken in in quick gulps?
Have you realized how this affects their speech, causing breathiness and quick gasps?
Can you remember what messages they gave out about themselves and how they made you feel?
Can you notice when *your* breathing reflects your tension?

Upper chest breathing is a reaction to arousal, but is also a trigger for the entire arousal response. If anxiety breathing becomes a habit, even when there is no special reason for it, the result is a person constantly in a state of alert with little control.

KEEP BREATHING

As I have explained, holding your breath is the tensing part of the breathing cycle. This is fine if the constant balance of inhaling and exhaling is maintained. If breath is held for over-long periods this either reflects stress already present or can induce a feeling of anxiety. If the muscles used in respiration are held in a state of tension, it is most likely that the other muscles in the body are tensing in sympathy. So while the breath-holding is being prolonged, the shoulders are probably pulling up and the face is setting into grim lines.

Many people get into the habit of holding their breath while doing tasks requiring concentration. I don't know what has caused this to arise, perhaps it is linked to being anxious about how well the task is done. I have noticed that I tend to hold my breath while trying to thread a needle. I hold the needle far away from me in an attempt to defy creeping middle age and deny my advancing long sight. Perhaps the breath-holding reflects an anxiety about the whole issue. Whatever the reason, it is important for me to break the habit, maintain calm by continuing to breathe both in and out – and resort to close-work spectacles!

Karen was very worried about her husband's frequent states of anxiety and depression which were casting a shadow over their home. On some mornings, when lying beside him, she could hear him holding his breath for a long period (sometimes 30–45 seconds), followed by a quick, noisy exhalation rapidly followed by an equally noisy gasping in of air. Then the holding would be repeated. She knew that this always heralded a bad day. His breathing was probably reflecting his mood but was also compounding the problem by causing him to start the day muscle-bound, and in a state of alert. What is more, she found herself mirroring his tension and had to consciously break free by making certain that at least she started the day breathing calmly, and relaxing her muscles every time she let her breath out.

Notice whether or not you hold your breath when concentrating hard.
Make certain that you breathe steadily in and out, letting yourself relax your muscles each time you breathe out.
Use your personal check list to relax your tension release triggers.
You might like to use some *inspeak* to explore the nature of your tension.

CALM NATURAL BREATHING

There is a difference between a *big* breath and a *deep* breath. A big breath draws in as much air as possible, filling the lungs to a great capacity. This is only needed for maximum effort and, if repeated too often, can cause hyperventilation. Now I understand why I experienced dizziness when, as a child, I followed my teacher's advice and took lots of big breaths at the freezing cold open window each morning. Big breaths should not be repeated more than once or twice without taking a rest. Calm, healthful breathing draws air deep down into the thorax (the chest cavity) while the shoulders remain dropped and the upper chest stays still. This is *deep breathing*. We need very little oxygen to function, as you will realize if you have ever learned mouth-to-mouth resuscitation. The small amount of oxygen that is 'wasted' as the resuscitator breathes out into the patient's mouth is sufficient to keep them alive, so we do not require a lot of air, but the small amount we do need should pass slowly, deep into our chests.

As you learn to control your breathing, you will find that you can consciously calm yourself and help your body to be more efficient. You can do this by 'pulling' the air in as you distend your abdomen and letting the air out as you flatten your abdominal muscles.

> Place a hand on your abdomen between the base of your ribs
> and your navel.
> Move your abdominal muscles to create a big bulge and
> then flatten again, causing your hand to move up and
> down.
> Make the action exaggerated to familiarize yourself with how
> your abdominal muscles can move.

EXERCISE 1

This is not really an exercise, but is an introduction to the experience of enjoying and practising calm, relaxed breathing. It is usually necessary to focus on it until it becomes the way you breathe most of the time. I describe this first so that you can become familiar with the desired outcome. It is helpful to recognize the ideal to which you aspire even if you find it difficult to achieve. The starter exercises and exercises 2 and 3 which follow may be useful tools to help you loosen and throw off tension before attempting exercise 1.

It is easiest to start while lying down. You should make yourself as comfortable as you can and be well supported. See that you are warm enough; perhaps you might like to cover yourself with a light blanket. Wear loose clothes, especially around your waist, chest and neck.

> Drop your shoulders and try to relax your body tensions.
> Let your breath out.
> Breathe in slowly and gently.
> Breathe out again, just as gently.
> *Take a fraction longer to breathe out than you did to breath in.*
> *Focus on letting yourself feel heavy and limp as you breathe out.*
> Pause and stay empty for a moment.
> Breathe in again and continue the cycle, allowing yourself
> gradually to slow down your rhythm.

While you are practising, you could, if you wish, place one hand on your upper chest in order to check that it is not heaving up and down and the other lightly on your abdomen to feel the gentle rising and falling back. If your abdominal muscles are moving, you are correctly using your diaphragm. Eventually you will not need to make these checks.

We can learn a lot from cats about how to relax. Imagine a cat sleeping on soft sand. If you were to lift the cat and look at the impression it had made in the sand, you would see that it extended to the full shape of its body with no gaps due to arched, tensed muscles. As you relax while breathing out it might be useful to try to emulate that totally relaxed cat. Imagine that you, too, are lying on soft sand and try, as you breathe out, to make a total impression with no gaps due to arched, tensed muscles. You could practise this exercise for at least five minutes a few times a day until it becomes the natural way you breathe when at rest. This not only helps you to relax your muscles, but has the effect of calming your pulse rate and, as a bonus, encourages endorphins (the body's own natural pain killers) to be released into your bloodstream. So slow, deep breathing is a gentle way of helping you to cope with pain or sickness. People suffering intractable pain sometimes find that they can give their pain threshold a lift by relaxed deep breathing which helps them to float over the pain.

If you see this exercise as a tyranny, and worry about how well you do it, this will cause the very tension that you are trying to avoid. So if positioning your breath is a problem, don't bully yourself. You are probably one of those people who prefer to focus instead on the cat in the sand and introduce yourself to relaxation through muscle responses. You are likely to find that your breathing calms down once you stop thinking about it!

Now is the time to start using gentle relaxed breathing when you are sitting and standing still. You can then experiment with breathing calmly while walking and performing actions.

STARTER EXERCISES

Sometimes you might find it hard to breathe calmly when you are conscious of exhibiting an anxious reaction. You can feel your heart pounding, your breath is fast and shallow and you are aware of needing some trick to get yourself started– a lead in to exercise 1, 2 or 3. A stretch and yawn might be all that you need. If something extra is required you could try one of the following:

The melting snowman

Imagine that you are a snowman standing in the garden.
It is icy cold and you are frozen stiff and solid.
Take in a big breath, hold it, and concentrate on what it feels like to be so rigid.
Now feel the warm sun on you.
Breathe out slowly as you melt.
Return to calm exercise 1 breathing.

Puppet on strings

Slowly take in a big breath as you imagine your strings pulling you rigid.
Feel yourself being stretched as your arms and legs are pulled up.
Say to yourself as you breathe in 'I think I can . . . I think I can . . . I think I can . . .'
As the strings slacken and you breathe out say to yourself with a sigh 'I . . . can . . .'
Return to calm exercise 1 breathing.
Try a slow or quick release and use whichever you prefer.

As big breaths are involved in both of these exercises, they should not be repeated immediately. If, after one or two attempts you are still finding difficulty calming yourself, take a break then try a *starter exercise* again.

EXERCISE 2

All the breathing exercises are based on the premise that breathing out induces relaxation, especially if accompanied by a conscious relaxing of muscles. The starter exercises and exercise 2 both use a sigh as a calming mechanism. But tense people also sigh a lot. The difference is that tense people tend to hold their breath and sigh intermittently. You know how important it is to keep breathing in order not to tense up again.

Starters are useful when you are alone, but exercise 2 is a simple 'quick soother' which you might need when in company. It is also a pleasurable reminder to use frequently throughout the day, a way of getting your breathing back on course.

Take in a slow big breath.
Put the tip of your tongue behind your bottom teeth.
Smile.
Drop your shoulders and –
Breathe out with a slow, gentle 'Hey . . .'

Return to calm regular breathing.

You might like to incorporate this type of breathing exercise into your collection of normal mannerisms. Test out the difference between drawing your breath in with a sharp 'ah' and letting it out with a gentle 'hey'.

CONQUER DISCOMFORT WITH YOUR BREATH

The slow release of air can be very helpful when anticipating uncomfortable or distressing procedures. Some people have a dislike of injections, of having blood tests or stitches removed. I shall use the blood test as an example.

Take in a *big* breath.
Drop your shoulders and let your hands stay unclenched and relaxed.
Start breathing out very, very, slowly so that you are still exhaling as the syringe is inserted.
Now maintain exercise 1 breathing.
Try to take your focus far away from the site of the anxiety so, for example, if your arm is involved, concentrate on relaxing your feet.

You might like to practise this technique in anticipation of the event. Test yourself to see how slowly you can let a gentle stream of air out and see if you can return to calm breathing instead of gasping air back in again.

EXERCISE 3

This is a method of slowly winding down which I enjoy when alone. It is an exercise that uses breathing and words in partnership. The phrase I like is 'I feel calm', but you might prefer to choose a phrase of your own. You may, in fact, be feeling far from calm. Don't worry about that; hopefully you will be calm by the time you have completed the exercise.

Drop your shoulders and relax all your muscles.
1 Take in a gentle breath.
2 As you breathe out say the words 'I feel calm'.
  Repeat steps 1 and 2 a few times, getting slower each time.
3 Say each word separately as you breathe out:
  Breathe in gently   Breathe out – ' I . . .'
  Breathe in gently   Breathe out – ' feel . . .'
  Breathe in gently   Breathe out – 'calm . . .'
  Repeat 3 getting slower and slower. You will probably find that you are leaving longer and longer periods between each word and that it becomes very pleasant to stay empty for rests before breathing in again.

As you become more and more familiar with these ways of controlling and enhancing your whole demeanour through using breathing techniques you will probably find they become second nature and you find many ways of applying them to your own personal situations. The tools you have learned should equip you to remain calm when you wish and to calm yourself when in difficult situations. I shall be referring back to them in future chapters as I deal with practical applications of relaxation.

CHAPTER 8

Deep Relaxation

THE LUXURY OF LETTING GO

You are now building up a range of techniques that can assist you to achieve the state of *deep relaxation*. You have started to identify muscle tensions as they begin; you have learned to apply your personal *tension release triggers* and have practised helpful breathing exercises. You are now ready to collect these skills together so that you can express the calm, serene aspects of yourself.

If you have been following the *tense–relax* exercise in chapter 6, the one that helps you to be aware of the difference between tension and relaxation in your muscles, you may be feeling a little frustrated by now. You will remember that, as you started to enjoy being comfortably relaxed, I suggested that you tense up again. I hope that you are recognizing the tensions, and you now deserve to reap the reward. You are ready to move on to the pleasure of relaxing deeply with no tension in any of your muscles.

SETTING ASIDE TIME

You deserve time for yourself! If you decide to grab your relaxing times only whenever appropriate gaps occur during the day, I suspect that they are unlikely to present themselves. If you want to be in control of your available time rather than a victim of circumstance, you may have to take a positive approach, to become active rather than reactive. Although relaxing before going to sleep is, of course, desirable, bedtime is not ideal for relaxation practice. The reason for this is that the aim of practising is not to send yourself to sleep. You need to consciously experience the sensation of being awake and yet pleasantly relaxed. Only if you are fully aware of this feeling can you apply it to day-to-day experiences.

How long your relaxing sessions should take must be decided by you. Setting aside 20 minutes is considered ideal, but many people find that 10 minutes fit better into their daily schedule. It is more beneficial to give yourself regular short sessions rather than rare long ones. What is important is that your appointed times should be respected both by you and others. You owe this to yourself.

When I had two young children around the house the words 'Mummy's time' were established very early in their vocabulary. I chose a time of day that came directly after I had been giving them a great deal of attention. I settled them down with activities appropriate to their age and took 10, increasing to 20, minutes of blissful *me-time*, stating firmly that I was not to be disturbed. (Obviously, I was not too far from them, just in case . . .) Firstly, I relaxed deeply, floating above the pressures of parenthood, then I used the remaining time to read. I am convinced that this equipped me to return to mothering without resentment and with renewed commitment.

> Rajiv was manager of a very busy insurance office. He was under pressure all his working day and this spilled over into his home, where he continued to be busy with the contents of his briefcase. After a heart attack he returned to work determined to make a few important changes. He established a new routine where he put a 'Do Not Disturb 'notice on his door for regular periods when he would use his newly acquired skill in deep relaxation. He then decided that, in addition, he was entitled to take a short lunch break without interruption by his staff or the telephone. On returning home, he treated himself to a relaxing time before confronting more work. He was delighted to find that his work did not deteriorate. In fact he tackled his duties with a new calm efficiency.

Setting aside time for deep relaxation is a good investment. It results in renewed energy and vigour. Once the skill is well established, even a very short time can have the desired effect. It takes courage to turn one's back, for example, on a mountain of plastic bags waiting to be unpacked after a visit to the supermarket and, instead, to relax deeply in an armchair for five minutes. But if the supermarket trek is the low spot of the week, the five-minute soother could become an invaluable time.

A period of deep relaxation before a trying time can set you up, giving you a necessary boost of energy; a similar period afterwards renews and refreshes. To plan both into your schedule is a luxury you may decide you want to give yourself.

What time of day will you set aside to practise deep relaxation?
What plans will you need to make to ensure that you are not disturbed?
Are there any distressful chores that you have to do that could be made more tolerable by taking a *five-minute soother* beforehand or afterwards?

PREPARATION FOR DEEP RELAXATION

Before settling down to a deep relaxation practice session, you might like to use some of the aids already mentioned in chapter 4. Breathing starter exercises, and breathing exercises 2 and 3, described in chapter 7 are a useful way in. Some people enjoy a simple massage of a particularly tense area. Here are a few massages that you could try:

1 Knead the muscles at the back of your neck. You will notice, as you press, that when your head is dropped forward, these muscles are tight. They are softest when your head is upright and gently balanced.
2 Place your hands round your head and move round, in both directions, as if you were trying to screw and unscrew a lid. Feel your scalp loosening.
3 Gently stroke your face with your fingertips, moving them up your nose, round your hair line and down your cheeks and sides of your neck.

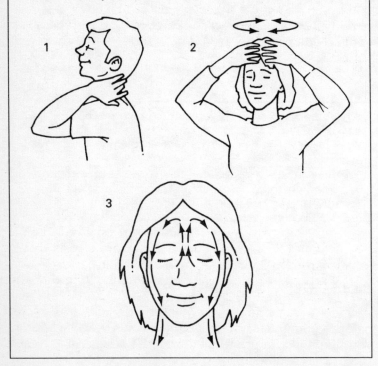

RELAX LYING DOWN

Make yourself comfortable. You can lie on a bed or on the floor but see that you are well supported. You might like to cover yourself lightly. You can experiment with relaxing on your back or, if you find this uncomfortable, on your side in the first aid 'recovery position'.

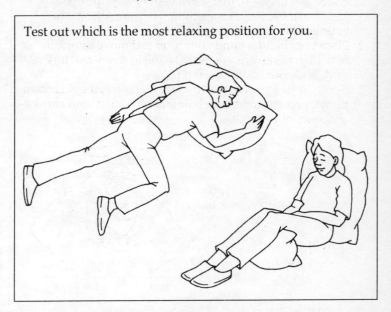

Test out which is the most relaxing position for you.

Use breathing exercise 1 and concentrate on relaxing each time you breathe out. Think of the cat on the sand and feel yourself getting heavy and limp. As you breathe out either say the word RELAX to yourself, or a word of your own or an increasingly slow phrase as in breathing exercise 3.

If you are new to the experience you may find that your *internal imp* tries to wreck things for you. You might get a twitch, a cramp or an itch. Don't worry about this. Just scratch or move to make yourself comfortable again and then settle back to continue relaxing. Eventually you could find that it is sufficient to acknowledge the discomfort but take no action. So you could say 'my leg itches' or 'my shoulder hurts' and then carry on relaxing. Surprisingly the discomfort frequently fades and your *imp* is subdued.

Feel yourself sinking down more and more and enjoy letting a warm heaviness engulf you. As you find yourself entering a deepening state of relaxation, you will probably feel yourself so calm and at rest that you will have a sensation of weightlessness and of time standing still.

If you are not using a cassette you might like to make a body scan to check that each part of you is relaxed. Go through your body from your feet upwards as in the tense/relax exercise in chapter 6 but this time, of course, leave out any tensing suggestions and focus only on letting each part of your body become relaxed and comfortable.

At the end of a relaxation session you might like to bring yourself back with a suggestion that could go something like:

> I am now going to count backwards from 5 to 1. When I reach 1, I will gently become aware of my surroundings, stretch, take in and release a big breath (breathing exercise 2), and then return to being alert with a clear head but still feel comfortably calm and relaxed. 5, 4, 3, 2, 1.

Then get up slowly, sitting briefly before getting into a standing position.

EMPTYING THE MIND

Unfortunately this is the greatest testing ground for you to tame your *internal imp*. Your personal inner saboteur takes the form of a *mental invader*. It is much easier to control your muscles than your thoughts. Repeating the word 'relax', (or your chosen word) on each exhalation can use up brain space to help exclude other thoughts. But the imp is cunning and those thoughts have a way of flowing back. There is no one solution for dealing with this problem so I will share with you some of the ploys that I have used and also some of the tricks that others have reported back to me.

- I like the Buddhist meditation teaching that helps to set thoughts in a proper place along a time scale. Your only concern must be the present. In the present, all that you are doing is breathing and relaxing your muscles, nothing else. So all other thoughts are either concerned with the past or the future. If the thought that creeps in is to do with the past, you can say to yourself, 'I am remembering'. If it is concerned with the future, then you can think 'I am planning'. As none of this is to do with now you can then nudge it to where it belongs, either back into the past or forwards into the future. Some people have suggested that replacing the word 'relax' with the word 'now' at such times might be useful.

- It may help to be open to thoughts as they come and go. Let them in; don't hold on to them; let them go. They are like clouds floating across the sky. Let them float away.

- If the thoughts are persistently knocking at the door of your mind, you might have to give them, at first, the attention they demand in the same way as you dealt with the physical interruptions that I have described earlier. The first stage is to acknowledge the *invader*; perhaps even analyse it. Then confirm that this is inappropriate right now as you are relaxing. So you might find yourself saying something like, 'I am thinking about the meeting I have to attend this afternoon, but this has nothing to do with now. Now I am relaxing!'

  You may find that you have to go one further and actually allocate a time to deal with the problem, and you might need to add to your *inspeak* something like, 'I will give the meeting my attention in 20 minutes when I have finished my relaxation session.'

- Those who like to use imagery might visualize collecting the thoughts in a box and setting it aside for another time, or putting the thoughts in a jug and pouring them away. Someone I know, who was enjoying her new video recorder used a mental 'fast forward' or 'fast backward' image to make short shrift of her *internal imp*.

- Listening to music or to a relaxation tape are popular ways of staying in the present.

- Sometimes the *imp* makes you focus on sounds around you that you know have nothing to do with you but seem to demand your attention. Simple uninvolved awareness may help to put them back into perspective. You could gently say, 'I hear . . . an aeroplane . . . a police car . . . a barking dog . . .' and then let them go.

It is better not to keep jumping from one method to another. Give yourself a chance to make your attempts work. If your internal imp looks like winning at the moment, the last thing you need is to add to your tension by feeling a failure. Stop worrying about it and try again another time. You might decide to have an internal conversation (see chapter 5) in order to find out what is troubling you. If you manage to find a method that suits you then stay with it and reject the rest.

RELAXING IN A CHAIR

Once you are ready to try a deep relaxation session in a sitting position you may have to consider how you will protect yourself from further invaders. If you are using a room in which you are usually active, it may be important to reaffirm your commitment to taking time for the session, to deal with the continuing demand of your imp and the demands for attention from others.

> Emma told me, when she moved from bed to chair, that she was invaded by annoyances in the room. Instead of leaping to her feet to deal with them, she resisted the temptation and decided to include in her inspeak 'I see a crooked picture . . . I see a smudge on the TV screen . . .' and was then able to let go of these thoughts as her attention gently drifted back.

Good sitting posture with a balanced head is more conducive to relaxation than a slumped or sprawling position with a drooped head. Sit well back in your chair with your spine supported and, if using an armchair, rest your arms lightly with your hands unclenched. You can advance through different stages to the challenge of being able to relax in an upright chair, sitting on a stool, or sitting on the floor. Experiment keeping your eyes closed at first and then opening them. When you start to keep your eyes open, focusing into the distance through a window can be relaxing. Let images just flow in and out of your awareness. You might find that you start discovering and appreciating new details around you which you were previously too busy to notice. Notice them – and let them go.

STAND AND RELAX

We tend to associate standing with action and movement and it takes some persistence to accept the notion that it is possible to stand and relax. It is, however, a very useful skill to acquire. You may decide to set aside time for this or you may prefer to stand for five minutes at the end of a sitting practice session. Check out your posture. Your weight should be evenly placed on the balls of both feet which should be slightly apart. Shoulders should be dropped and level, and hips should also be level. Let your head stay gently balanced and your arms and hands relaxed by your sides. All the comments about attention when relaxing while sitting will apply also when you are relaxing while standing.

FOCUSING ON ONE PART OF THE BODY

Sit comfortably with one hand lightly placed palm upwards on your lap.
Drop your shoulders and breathe out a relaxing 'hey' (breathing exercise 2).
Look at your hand and concentrate on its feeling heavy and warm.
Say 'heavy' and 'warm' to yourself as you focus on your hand.
Notice any changes in sensation in your hand.
Notice any changes in the way you feel generally.

Many people find that they experience a tingling sensation in their hands. This means that they have relaxed so much that they can feel blood pulsating through their fingers. (Some of them are even able to count their pulse rate in this way.) Thinking of heaviness seems to induce the opposite, and some people report a sense of lightness or just weight-lessness. This sensation is often more intense when focused on one hand, but can indicate what a truly deep relaxed state can feel like. Once established, it is often possible to let this sensation spread throughout the body and some people have found it a useful aid to entering a deep relaxation session. They find that if one bit goes, it all goes.

> Audrey was an 'A' level student who always had the jitters on entering an examination room. She learned to calm her twitching muscles, pounding heart and fast, shallow breathing by allowing herself a few calming moments when she relaxed her hand which she placed on the desk in front of her. She found that, with practice, she induced the required response very quickly. The few minutes used up before turning over the examination paper were a good investment as she was then able to apply herself to the task with alertness and a clear head.

THE QUICK SOOTHER

It would be a pity if you were able to use only lengthy relaxation sessions. Once you become familiar with the sensation of letting go of tensions you will probably dis-cover the value of the *quick soother*. You get into a deeply relaxed state in exactly the way you would for a lengthy practice, either lying down, sitting or standing – whichever is appropriate. You then enjoy a quick relaxation which may last for only a few minutes, but will allow you to take the opportunity to recharge your batteries in any way that fits into your personal lifestyle. You may consciously need to allow this habit into your day. You could take advantage of natural breaks in the day: before going out, on arriving at home or at work, before or after meals, after finishing a task or before beginning a new one. Times that could potentially be tensing might be converted into welcome challenges to test your ability to relax: waiting in a queue, a traffic jam or a waiting room. Once you have incorporated the *quick soother* into your day you will be amazed at the extra energy you generate.

IMAGERY

The use of imagery can be a very pleasant way of unwinding. Remember which of the senses speak most eloquently to you and use them creatively. If you are a visual person you might imagine a favourite, or fantasy, place of serenity. Inside your mind anything goes, so you can really enjoy your visit, making certain that you truly unwind in that place. If it helps you, add sounds and aromas that please you. Tactile imagery can be deeply soothing. You might imagine the sensation of being rocked or stroked. You might drift gently in a boat or on a raft, or imagine yourself flying or swimming. If you prefer to be led in your imagery you could use a 'visualization' tape.

This chapter has introduced you to the techniques involved in relaxing deeply in specially set aside sessions. I hope that you will join those of us who firmly believe that the time involved is worthwhile. You are now ready to widen the application of these skills so that you can reduce distress in normal day-to-day activities.

CHAPTER 9

Applied Stress Control

STAY COOL AND SUCCEED

'It's hard to keep an even pace, but slow and steady wins the race!' This sentence remains emblazoned in my child-hood memories as, at regular intervals throughout the play depicting the well-known fable of the 'hare and the tortoise', I repeated them in my theatrical debut at the age of seven. I crawled across the stage weighed down by a cumbersome shell strapped to my back. I think I was miscast as the tortoise, finding it easier to identify with the mercurial hare. But I get the point. However, I think that although 'slow and steady' may be the best route for some, it is only one of many ways to stay calm and succeed. We each have a right to be true to ourselves and to employ forms of stress management that are self-enhancing.

As in other chapters, I recommend that you use suggest-ions that make sense to you and reject the rest. I hope that you will discover that the application of stress management skills day-to-day will keep you in control of your life, aid efficiency, and maximize energy and enjoyment.

SPECIFIC TENSION

In the *tense/release* exercises (chapter 6) you were required to tense only one set of muscles at a time while leaving the rest of your body relaxed. This is a useful reminder to you that it is not necessary to tense up completely every time muscles are used. It is easy to get into bad habits: hunching shoulders when only the muscles of the hand and arm need to work, screwing up face muscles, gnashing teeth, frowning while concentrating on the job in hand. The act of tensing up muscles uses energy. If this is done unnecessarily the result is more likely to be fatigue and a greater difficulty in unwinding afterwards. You will seldom need to use all your muscles at any one time, they are tools which serve you well when used selectively. Specific tension is using only those muscles that are required for a task. It is economical with your effort, and you can then return to rest once the tools are no longer needed. You will find that it is also easier to keep a clear head if all redundant muscles are relaxed.

Lift a pen and write a few words on a piece of paper.
Notice that you can use the muscles in your hand and arm without having to tense the rest of your body.
Put the pen down and let go of the tension in your hand and arm. Feel them relax as soon as the task is completed.

Hold the telephone and be aware of the specific tensions required.
Speak into the mouthpiece so that you are now using the muscles of your face in addition to those in your hand and arm. Check that your shoulders and your other hand remain relaxed.
Replace the telephone and stop talking.
Be aware of relaxing after your muscle tensions are no longer needed.

The essentials of *specific tension* are:

- Use only the muscle groups required for a task.
- Check that all redundant muscles are comfortably at rest.
- Release the muscle tensions as soon as the task is done.

Soon you will notice that you can walk about while keeping your face, shoulders, hands and arms comfortably relaxed; you will be able to use your hands without tensing up your face; you will be able to look around you while keeping the rest of your body relaxed and you will be able to concentrate on your activities without frowning. Once you have developed this awareness you will no doubt collect your own examples of using specific tension to advantage while keeping the rest of yourself calm and at rest. Remember the importance of letting go of those useful tensions as soon as the task is completed.

TRANSITIONAL RELAXATION – SWEEP AWAY THE CRUMBS

Tension has a nasty way of creeping up on us. We accumulate the debris of muscle tension and anxiety that accompanies each task we do. As the day progresses, we become so cluttered up that it gets harder and harder to face each new activity with the calm alertness that it deserves. By the end of the day, we could be so overwhelmed that it might be difficult to unwind. We may find we cannot easily let go of these thoughts which chase themselves around our minds, sometimes into the night.

How do good cooks prepare a meal?
Firstly, they start with a clean work surface.
The grapefruits are cut and portioned.
The table is now covered with pips and juice, so this is wiped clean.
The vegetables are sliced up, and again the table is cleaned.
This cleaning of the work surface between each different activity is a basic hygiene procedure and prevents crumbs from one dish getting mixed up in the next.

We have a tendency to let the residue of experiences hang around to spill over into the rest of the day. We carry accumulated body tensions, often we hold on to our thoughts and feelings, and sometimes we try a 're-run', going over and over an event (even trying to mentally rewrite the script to alter the outcome). We owe it to ourselves to enjoy each part of the day and to greet each challenge with energy and alert anticipation. If we are aiming at mental hygiene we, too, must clear away the crumbs so that we can face each new experience with a clean work surface.

Here is an exercise which exaggerates the *wipe clean* process:

Take a simple scenario. You are sitting in a room. Your coat is placed on the other side of the room. From the chair you walk over to your coat, put it on, walk round the room, replace your coat, return to your chair and sit down.

Now divide the exercise up into its smallest components. Between each part you will stand and breathe out, drop your shoulders and briefly relax. Use a *quick soother* technique, letting a wave of relaxation flow over you and breathe out with an exercise 2 'Hey' . . . either aloud or to yourself. The pattern will be: activity – pause (breathe out and relax).

```
Sit – Relax
   Stand – Relax
      Walk to your coat – Relax
         Pick up your coat – Relax
            Put your coat on – Relax
               Walk round the room – Relax
                  Stand still – Relax
                     Take the coat off – Relax
                        Put the coat down – Relax
                           Walk to your chair – Relax
                              Stand – Relax
                                 Sit – Relax
```

Try it again, making the relax times very short but effective. Do you notice how you are able to focus on your activities with a new intensity and awareness?

Anxiety often results from trying to focus on more than one thing at a time. Here, you are learning to allow each activity to be of the utmost importance while it is being done and then letting it go, leaving the work surface clean and ready for whatever comes next. I have been told by people trying *transitional relaxation*, that they have found their concentration is much improved and their appreciation of their actions much enhanced. This was explained by Charles:

> As I focused on peeling potatoes, I found myself looking at the tuber as if I had never seen it before. It really was quite amazing – the texture of the skin, the position of the buds, the shapes made as the skin pared off. Then I shifted my focus to the potato peeler. What a clever piece of engineering! I was then tempted to start examining my hands but that would probably take up too much time and is a delight that will be postponed.

The exercise is exaggerated and I am not suggesting that you adopt a start–stop approach to the day. I do hope, however, that you will allow yourself to pause sufficiently to shake off accumulated tensions and be mindfully involved in whatever you are doing. You may find, as a bonus, that you have fewer memory lapses and a lower accident rate.

You might manage to incorporate a relaxing exhalation and quick tension release each time you sit down so that it becomes habitual – sit . . . drop shoulders . . . 'hey' . . . You could then use transitional relaxation in other natural breaks to stop yourself charging from one activity to the next. If you are a *re-run* person you might need to look at how you can let go of events that you would wish to have altered. It takes courage to be able to say to yourself, 'That really hurt me' or 'That isn't how I wanted to react' or 'I didn't handle that as well as I would wish.' Then, after accepting the reality, perhaps you could attempt to forgive yourself, deal with the frustration of knowing that it has gone, that you are not perfect and might react differently next time.

ONE THING AT A TIME

> Helen is a very active person. Whenever I ask her how she is, she replies, 'You know me – busy, busy, busy!' She is so busy

that while she speaks to me on the telephone I can hear her tapping on her computer or rattling pots and pans. She talks while she eats, while she reads, invariably spills the milk, doesn't remember what she has eaten, and has no recollection of any conversations or plans she's agreed to. My first reaction is to feel that I am not important enough for her to give me her full attention. When I think again I realize that this is really about how she sees herself and has little to do with me. If she were to allow herself some *inspeak*, she might discover that she values herself not in relation to what she *is* but only what she *does*.

Helen, actually, doesn't achieve more than the rest of us. She is inefficient, over-anxious and exhausted – and she certainly isn't a bundle of laughs!

The consequence of *transitional relaxation* is that it really pays off as it helps us to focus on the activity in hand. If we can ensure that we stay with only one thing at a time we will benefit from being able to concentrate more fully. As a bonus we will give ourselves a calming message and present a more pleasing aspect to others.

In our day-to-day encounters it is essential for good interpersonal relations that we give people our complete attention when they speak to us. If you have ever met a professional, perhaps a doctor or a manager, who has not made eye contact and has dealt with you while writing, making asides to another person, or using the telephone, you will know how this leaves you feeling ill at ease, and how destructive it can be to the relationship.

Students may find the 'one thing at a time' principle of value as an aid to concentration. It is so easy to slip guiltily into the habit of never being free of the permanently open book. The sight of the book becomes a constant reminder, a symbol of the problem, but doesn't solve it. So much more can be learned if periods are set aside for concentrated study, however short. It is most important that study time has recognized limits.

When I was a student I was tempted to spend many hours with an open book on my lap – daydreaming! After I gave myself permission to spend time walking on the seafront or rambling on the South Downs – or even just going to bed early – I found that I could return to my work with a fresh approach, tension healed, and I worked quickly and well.

This isn't just advice for students. How many of you, I wonder, feel guilty if you take time out for a while. Sometimes it is necessary to be resolute in getting off the treadmill, confident that when you return to the task in hand you will experience *quality time* with an extra surge of energy and concentration to do well. What you are doing is replacing damaging chronic stress with a short burst of adrenaline which is both exciting and, researchers report, physically good for you. So you could call it *quality stress*! You are making an active decision to:

Stop – Stand back – Enjoy yourself

and then get back to work.

AFFIRMATIONS AND KEY WORDS

Being in a state of deep relaxation makes a person more responsive to suggestion. You can make suggestions to yourself when in a relaxed state if you want to affect the way you feel once you are up and active again. A good time is at the end of a relaxation session, just before opening your eyes. You can choose statements that can be used in a number of ways:

- you could decide to re-inforce the state of calm that you want to continue feeling throughout the day.
- you might want to increase your confidence and affirm your own abilities.
- you might want to promote a particular feeling about yourself that will help you achieve a special objective.

For whatever reason you choose to use affirmation statements there are guidelines that are worth following:

Always keep your statements positive
  Forget negative punishing phrases. So there will be no 'I
  can't, I won't, I am not . . .' Throw disbelief to the wind
  and act as if what you are saying is really true. For
  example, say 'I am truly calm!' At this stage your internal
  imp will probably interrupt with 'Oh no you're not!' Deal
  with your imp in whatever way suits you – lock it away,
  stuff a banana in it's mouth – just keep on believing.

Keep your statement in the present
  This applies even if it refers to a future time. You are
  saying something that you want to take on board about
  yourself now so there is no room for 'I want to, I wish, I
  will.' So, instead of 'I will feel confident at the interview,' you say, 'I am confident at interviews.' Instead of,
  'I want to give up smoking,' try 'I breathe fresh air. I am
  free of nicotine.'

Select sentences or phrases that are short and snappy and
perhaps have some lyrical quality. Here are a few you
might like to choose from:

  I feel calm. / I am quietly confident. / I speak clearly and
  confidently. / Now I am achieving . . . / Learning is
  something I enjoy hugely. / I am comfortable in company.
  / I think effectively and efficiently. / My mind is alert
  and creative.

Think up some phrases for yourself. They will be more
effective if they are tailor-made.
  In your relaxed state, say your affirmations quietly to
yourself. I am a great advocate of speaking aloud, but if this
worries you, it may all have to happen inside your head.
You will probably need to repeat your affirmation four or
five times in order to beat your imp. You will be surprised
to discover that the statement becomes increasingly
credible as you repeat it.

I can do it.	Imp: No I can't
I can do it.	Imp: Well, perhaps I can
I *can* do it.	Imp: Possibly I can
I can do it.	Imp: Well, all right, I can

Once your statement has been programmed in you can easily re-enforce it by repeating it after a *quick soother* at appropriate times during the day. Instead of using a statement, you might enjoy having a special word that has a private message for you. It might be helpful to associate it with an action that is your coded message to yourself.

Winston wanted to overcome his shyness. In company he clammed up, avoided contact and clenched his fists, which he felt symbolized his feeling of vulnerability and the need to hold tight to himself. He very much wanted to risk being able to open out in company. He chose 'open' as a key word and decided to accompany it with a private sign of unclenching and opening his hand. He prepared a few sentences to end his relaxation session to suggest every time he said the key word 'open' and spread his fingers he felt supremely confident and able to enjoy the contact of others. He eventually preferred using the sign alone, as for him action was more eloquent than words.

Some people like using small objects or amulets which they can handle or look at to help them through tense moments. Think of the popularity of worry beads, car mascots, favourite cushions and old beloved cuddly toys.

REHEARSAL

If you are a worrier who goes through anticipated anxiety-provoking situations in your mind, you could be a good candidate for *positive rehearsal*. Worriers approach difficult times over and over in their minds. The situation gets no better and the distress increases; they give themselves a bad time. If you have the ability to plan ahead, you might as well use this skill to make life more comfortable for yourself. So turn the process on its head. Your punishing anticipation can become a positive planning to test out how you would like the encounter to proceed.

Set aside time to think about the forthcoming event.

Give yourself a period of deep relaxation and resist the temptation to start worrying. Tell yourself that there will be plenty of planning time later. Once you are relaxed, take yourself through the dreaded event stage by stage. At each stage soothe away any tension. Behave in a way that will help you to deal with it successfully. If you find it useful, you can talk yourself through, remembering to keep all your comments positive and in the present. You may wish to introduce key words or affirmation statements to support your rehearsal. When you have completed your mental experience say to yourself something like 'I have done it!' Give yourself praise for your success.

Your newly acquired stress-coping skills have now graduated from the relaxation sessions to the big wide world. You will find you have new techniques which can be applied in those day-to-day activities which, in the past, contributed to your accumulated stress. By nipping tensions in the bud and dealing with them as they arise you will find that the big build-up problems are presenting themselves less and less. You will begin to respond to the small smoulderings rather than wait for total burn-out.

CHAPTER 10

Functional Stress Management

FACE THE WORLD BUT STILL
STAY CALM

The stage is now set. You are ready in your make-up and costume. You have rehearsed until you feel that your performance is word perfect. But this is the big one. This is the real thing. As you step on to the stage can you make the character your own? Can you actually become the character? Unlike the stage performance, however, you do not want to take on a false personality. Your rehearsals, I hope, have led you to acquire the skills to be an enhanced and more comfortable you. Let us now look at the ways in which your hard work can help you to be capable of calmly coping with the real stresses in your life.

GREET SLEEP WITH PLEASURE

Sleep patterns are very personal; think of the natural and spontaneous sleeping rhythms of children and animals. Unfortunately we often feel pressurized by the need to conform with others. There can be demands to synchronize with family members and with society generally, and we can very easily allow ourselves to become stressed by the frustration of not fitting in.

Let me emphasize that there is no right or wrong, only right or wrong for *you*. So firstly get to know yourself.

Do you need a lot of sleep or a little?
Are you a lark or an owl? Do you know at which times you are most or least alert?
Is it better for you to have short cap naps rather than one long sleep?
Do you sleep better sitting up, lying in bed or elsewhere?

Forget what you ought to do, there are no rules. Your sleep is for you and you alone. If necessary you may need to talk this through with your partner or family members and some negotiation may be required.

Ivor was plagued by sleepless nights. He was annoyed to find that he regularly curled up on the settee during the evening and slept well. Once 'bed-time' arrived and he transferred to his bed, he was wide awake again. He decided to stop feeling anxious about this, to wrap himself in a duvet and spend the nights on his settee. The experiment worked. He was then able to choose whether to adopt this permanently or to return to his bed once a good sleep rhythm had been established.

Sonya was a teacher who found that her need to take an afternoon nap seriously interfered with her work. Her evenings were marred by accumulated fatigue and gave her no pleasure. She went to the extreme lengths of changing her work pattern, and she was lucky enough to be able to find a morning teaching post. In the evenings, once she discovered the joy of a second wind, she taught in night school.

It isn't always possible to be as flexible as Sonya, but perhaps it might be worth looking at ways of compromising in order to honour your needs. Remember that an hour of deep relaxation could be more refreshing than a whole tension-tossed night.

Preparing for sleep

It is useful to establish a routine that helps you to wind down towards sleep. So, avoid any mental stimuli such as quarrels or holiday plans. Allocate another time to deal with these things.

- A warm milky drink or calming herb tea can aid relaxing. Some people find tea or coffee over-stimulating.
- A small amount of alcohol may help you sleep. A large amount is likely to knock you out, but is unhelpful as it provides a drug-induced sleep which is not beneficial and may cause a hangover.
- Some people need a little extra exercise before going to bed and find walking the dog relaxing; others find the cool night air too stimulating.
- Sex, if satisfying, aids sleep; if unsatisfactory it has the opposite effect. If sex is currently a problem, bedtime may not be the best time of day to try to solve it.
- Always allow a calm time before going to bed – listen to music or have a deep relaxation session. If you are reading, try to avoid cliff-hangers.

A useful massage to help you get to sleep

Lie face downwards on your bed with your partner kneeling beside you. With both hands flat, your partner should push hard up the centre of your back and round to the sides – and repeat this movement a few times. Then, using finger tips, your partner should gently stroke your back, from the head downwards with alternate hands, keeping the contact continuous (only removing one hand when the other is in contact). Move gently to your sleeping position and continue for a while.

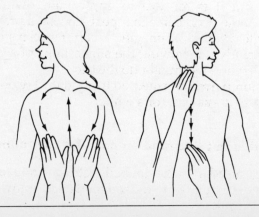

- You might like to try a few drops of calming essential oils, such as lavender, on your pillow.

If you lie awake or waken in the night . . .

Reassure yourself that it doesn't matter if you don't fall asleep. Lying in bed pleasantly relaxed can be just as good for you. So don't get anxious because you are still awake. This will only get you into a state of arousal which is the opposite of relaxation. Concentrate on enjoying being awake and deeply relaxed. You might say to yourself something like, 'Sleep doesn't matter. I am calm and relaxed and that is good for me.'

At one time I found myself waking in the early hours of the morning. I greeted the opportunity of not having to get up immediately and bounce into action. I enjoyed just lying there listening to the dawn chorus, a delight usually denied me and I found I was soon asleep again. But even if I had not slept, the rest would have been sufficient. It is only agitated sleeplessness that causes us to start the day tired and fretful.

Employ any of the techniques for muscle relaxation, relaxed breathing and emptying the mind that you have found most useful. Many people have told me that they find breathing exercise 3 (I feel calm) to be especially helpful, but it is for you to apply your own favourite routine. Some people like to repeat a poem, a prayer, some meaningless sound or imagine a very familiar place or an imaginary idyll. Following the suggestions of a relaxation or visualization tape might do the trick.

Don't jump from one method to another. Try one method and stick to it – at least for a while.

If you still can't sleep and cannot calm your mind . . .

It is not helpful to lie in bed getting more and more distressed. Get up, go to the toilet, make a hot water bottle or have a drink.

If thoughts are chasing round in your mind and will definitely not be tamed, make some brief notes or record them on a tape recorder (a few key words, written or spoken, will probably be sufficient to convince you that you can take up the issues in more detail the following day). Then get back to allowing yourself to be calmly comfortable again.

If you wake in a panic, you are probably high on your own hormones after an arousing dream. You may need to reassure yourself (aloud if necessary) that thoughts get distorted in the night. You will then have the tedious task of settling yourself down again. Remember that it takes much longer to calm down than to get aroused so you will have to be patient with yourself.

Sangeeta was a busy mother of three. She was experiencing severe sleeping difficulties and decided to experiment with a re-training method. If she was awake after 15 minutes in bed, she would get up, no matter how tired she felt, and carry out some activity for 5 to 10 minutes. Then she could go back to bed. If, after 15 minutes, she was still awake she would repeat the process. In fact she had to continue to get up all night if necessary. The function of this exercise was to re-train herself to associate bed with sleep and not to connect bed with being awake.

She kept a record of her experiences: night 1 – she got up six times; night 2 – three times; night 3 – once; night 4 – slept all night.

She used the waking times to do her French homework. This was a chosen activity that she seldom found time for during the day. She started to allocate more time for herself during the day, even if it meant giving her family the occasional 'fast' dinner. She continued to sleep well.

Sangeeta chose a very harsh regime for herself but she was confident that it was right for her.

It is your responsibility to chose for yourself a method with which you feel comfortable. Whichever way you decide to help yourself to attain a peaceful night's sleep, stay with it and allow it to become an important part of your life.

Have a good night!

ANXIETY PROVOKING SITUATIONS

When better to apply self-calming than when challenged by a distressing situation? Your body has signalled 'tensions'; your *inspeak* has interpreted 'trouble'. You are now ready to utilize this awareness in a creative way.

It is reassuring to check your ability to cope with the distress in a safe environment before having a head-on confrontation, so I shall suggest a few testers that might stir up a slight level of anxiety to enable you to practise.

Relax to let go of any current tensions.
Let yourself imagine dealing with each of the following situations in turn.
Feel the tension and recognize how you react.
Use a quick soother to calm yourself. Take as long as you need until you are confident that you have returned to your original state of relaxation.
1   You are putting cereal into a bowl. Suddenly, you see that the milk on the stove is boiling over.
2   You are leaving your home when you come face to face with a neighbour you quarrelled with last week.
3   As you approach your car you see a parking ticket on the windscreen.

Now you are ready to test your ability to calm yourself in imaginary situations that could cause a higher level of anxiety. If there is any personal reason why you may find one of these too upsetting, don't try to do it. Make up a new scene that you feel you can tolerate.

---

1   You are standing on the platform as the train pulls away. You remember you have left your briefcase on board.
2   You have spent hours trying to repair a domestic appliance. You are at a crucial last stage requiring a steady grip, when the dog knocks it from your hand.
3   You have just received some disturbing news by telephone. You do not want your children to know at present that you are upset.

Make certain that you leave sufficient deep relaxation time between each tension tester. You will learn to recognize when you are really calm again. Some people like to take their pulse before the tester; they note how it has risen when they are anxious and check to see that it has returned to their normal resting rate.

You are now ready to consider real life situations. There are no 'oughts' or 'shoulds'. What causes you distress may be completely different from things that bother other people. You might, first, like to give yourself a trial run just to reassure yourself that, when it occurs, you will be on top of the situation rather than a victim of pressure.

Think of a situation that regularly causes you to tense up.
Imagine it as if it is happening in the present.
Allow yourself to focus on the place and the people involved.
Be conscious of what is happening and what is being said.
Recognize your tension triggers which tell you that you are beginning to feel uncomfortable.
STOP.
STEP BACK.
Use the calming exercises that you find most helpful.
Clear your thoughts briefly.
Use *inspeak* to sort out what you want to do.
Use any statements, key words or actions that help.
Now deal with the situation knowing you're on top of it.

Now try it with other examples.
Grade your trials starting with those easily dealt with.
As your confidence grows you can graduate to more demanding events.

You have had a trial run and are ready to face the real world.

If you know in advance that a scary scene is about to take place you start at an advantage. If, for example, you are about to walk into an examination or interview room, or are going to speak in public, or know you will shortly come face to face with someone in a difficult encounter, you are in the fortunate position of being able to prepare yourself. If possible, take yourself to a private place for a few calming moments. The toilet, or rest room, may have to fulfil this function, and is no bad place. You can lock the door, sit down and take as long as you need with no one demanding your attention. This is not the time for rehearsal. If you have used rehearsal as a form of preparation it should have been done before now. Going over and over what you want to do is more likely to cause strain at this stage and will impede concentration.

> Peter, although well prepared for his examination, started to doubt his ability to think clearly under exam conditions. He decided to learn by rote the answers to expected questions. When he faced his question paper he was so tense from repeating his model answers to himself that he rapidly set down the prepared scripts without standing back to consider the paper in a relaxed way. Unfortunately, he read what he wanted to see and not what was there, and produced a well-planned, but inappropriate, paper – and failed.

If you allow yourself to go blank just long enough to become relaxed, you will be much more alert and thoughts will flow more easily. I know this is hard to believe, and it takes courage to let go of a rehearsed script. Your trust in your own coping ability will truly be put to the test. So why not try it out first in small unimportant situations in order to build up confidence?

If you are caught up in a pressurized scene and have not had any warning, then you may need to remove yourself for a few calming moments if it is at all possible.

> Jane felt herself becoming increasingly agitated as she tried to tell the builders that they were not carrying out her instructions correctly. Their responses were aggressive and uncivil. She felt her muscles tensing and her voice becoming shrill. Suddenly she stopped and said, 'I have to go inside for a moment but I'll be back.' She did a *quick soother*, emptied her mind briefly, collected her thoughts and then confronted her builders with calm determination.

If you are not able to distance yourself from a situation you will have to get a grip on things there and then. Remember that you don't have to respond with alacrity to what is happening around you. There is no harm done if you are ponderous. You will be more in control if you can allow yourself time to pause and quickly calm yourself.

Anxiety! – Stop – relax muscles as you breathe out with a slow sigh (breathing exercise 2) – take your time as you take action.

You could employ delaying tactics while assessing the situation and have a quick internal conversation. Let me remind you of delaying phrases suggested in chapter 5, 'Well, let me see . . .' 'Hmm . . . so what seems to be happening is . . .' 'Hey . . . so what you're saying is . . .'

> I allowed myself time to calm down twice lately. Once, when I had slipped on an icy pavement and felt shaken, I resisted the temptation to spring back into action and sat on the curb until I felt sufficiently composed to get up slowly. To the person who rushed to my aid I said, 'I would like just to sit still for a moment.' When a minor car collision left me feeling slightly shocked, I again felt the need to respond by sitting quietly in the car for a few minutes before getting out and facing the task of surveying the damage, attributing blame and exchanging phone numbers. I said quietly that I was not badly hurt, but wanted to sit still for a few moments. Using relaxation techniques, I only delayed proceedings by about a minute!

If you need time to calm down you have a right to take it. As you can't expect others to read your mind, you must take the responsibility yourself for getting what you want. As you perfect the technique you will be amazed to find that the amount of time involved may be very short indeed.

THE GENTLE WAY WITH PAIN AND SICKNESS

There are many benefits from the practice of deep relaxation as an aid to healing. When the body is in a state of arousal, the additional adrenaline present slows down cell repair and renewal. Relaxation works on the para-sympathetic nervous system which counters this and allows repair to continue. As I have said before, as the body relaxes, endorphins are released which act as a natural analgesic and increase a sense of well-being. Relaxing deeply has been found to lower blood pressure and, as it can result in a slower pulse, can help reduce bleeding. (If you are taking any medication that affects the metabolism, as with diabetes, you may find that your needs may alter and this should be checked with your medical adviser.)

If you are sick it is more important to allow yourself time to relax so that you can release sufficient energy to aid recovery. You can also employ your choice of techniques to deal with the pain and discomfort. It is a paradox that by relaxing in the face of discomfort you can actually become comfortable.

Here are a few ideas for you to try when you are in pain:
Acknowledge the pain. Be aware of how it is important to you at the moment; the pain is part of you right now.
Use your own favourite type of imagery to care for the pain:

If you are visual, perhaps think of its colour and gradually make the colour softer, less harsh. Think of the shape of the pain and let its outline blur.
If you are aural, hear the sound – perhaps a scream or a thudding – and try to let it become softer, gentler, slower.
If you are tactile, feel the rhythm: stabbing, throbbing, dull and continuous. Try to think of warming or stroking it, washing it or spreading it away. Let yourself sway or rock with the rhythm.

You may prefer to take your attention away from the discomfort:
Focus on deeply relaxing a part of the body far from the hurt area; for example, think of a warm, heavy foot while at the dentist.
Use your own imagery to take your attention elsewhere – look out of the window or at a picture, listen to music or the radio.

Have you noticed that when people are feeling contented and distress-free they have a glow of good health about them? It seems to be true that good stress management can seriously improve your health!

DRIVING AND OTHER TASKS

I am using driving as an example of how you can approach most of your day-to-day activities with a calm control. It will be for you to apply the salient features for your own purposes and your own personal situations.

- Be aware of how you see your car. Is it a status symbol? Is it a means of expressing your power or aggression? Is it simply a convenient vehicle for getting you from one place to the next?
- Plan your route before setting out.
- Get in slowly. Take a brief time to settle yourself, adjusting mirror and seat. Relax with a quick soother for half a minute with both feet on the floor and your hands on your lap. Half a minute, when relaxing, feels like a much longer time and is most beneficial.
- Care for your posture. You should be seated with your legs slightly bent. If you have to brake suddenly, your bent leg can absorb the shock. Keep your shoulders dropped and your back well supported.
- As you drive, keep your left foot on the floor rather than poised over the pedal.
- Hold the steering wheel lightly. Hook your thumbs over the spokes gently.
- Have regular tension checks of your hands, shoulders, jaw and forehead (road junctions or traffic lights provide good natural breaks for checks).
- Keep your vision wide.
- Listen to music provided this does not distract you. A relaxation cassette may cause you to be less alert, so best avoid it.

- Make sure you have enough fresh air.
- Eat small snacks rather than a heavy meal. On a long journey, keep some nibbles or a drink to hand.
- Pump your feet up and down occasionally while waiting at traffic lights to keep your circulation active and, if the journey is long, get out and walk around for a moment once every hour.
- If you feel drowsy, always pull in and have a deep relaxation session. You can't afford not to!
- Avoid the use of a car telephone while you are on the move. If you receive calls, develop the policy of stating that you will phone back once you can pull over and park.
- Use any delays for a quick relaxation practice. Welcome the opportunity.

Look at the tense faces of the other drivers and congratulate yourself on getting it right!

> Write out (or talk through) a plan for any other activity for yourself.
> Make certain that you are allowing for your physical comfort.
> Include the provision of time for calming and resting.

You owe it to yourself to make your life as comfortable as possible. I do hope that however onerous the experience, you are allowing yourself to perceive it as a challenge which can have some positive and pleasurable aspects for you. Even if the task remains horrid, you can enjoy the satisfaction of having been successfully skilful.

CHAPTER 11

The Way Ahead

GETTING THE BALANCE RIGHT

The path ahead of you is full of adventure and challenges. You are well-prepared to give yourself a good balance of relaxation, recreation and creative stress, and are ready to approach the future with the ability to make plans and to assure your own success and self-fulfilment.

A POSITIVE APPROACH

We all know people who see the world as a dangerous place, who see themselves as victims and are readily available to receive hurts. Because of this perception of their lives, they indulge in 'poor me' talk and continue to pile further distress on themselves. Perhaps we have all fallen into this self-destructive trap from time to time, so we know how easily, once we start, we find ourselves getting deeper and deeper into the pit. Once we decide to give up the role of the hunted prey we can find the courage to survive the pitfalls and partake fully of all our experiences.

Change the Perception

Helga and Albert live on a busy street. Whenever Albert attempts to back his car out of their drive, he finds the wait for a convenient gap in the traffic intolerable. He clings to the fantasy that he should be able to get away immediately, is therefore disappointed, and always starts his journey with anger, discontent and muscle tensions. Helga has different expectations. She allows sufficient time and assumes that it will take about five minutes to drive on to the road. Generally she is away long before that time and starts her working day always pleasantly suprised relaxed.

Sometimes, just by changing the vocabulary you might find that you can influence the way you feel. No doubt you have heard the examples of differing perception demonstrated by whether you say that the bottle of wine is half empty or half full, of seeing danger as a challenge, or of seeing potential risk as an adventure. I once heard a lonely lady refer to her apartment as 'the four walls'. She would feel differently if she perceived it as her haven rather than her prison. A man who reported that he had a bad night had, in fact, visited the bathroom three times and then slept soundly again.

It is a help if you can get into the habit of using objective rather than judgmental statements about yourself. You can stop thinking of yourself as 'stupid', 'incompetent', 'lazy', 'a failure' and instead start saying, 'I don't understand that', 'I didn't do that well', 'I didn't try hard enough', 'I failed that exam'. You will begin to understand that you are responsible for your behaviour, but you are not the sum total of what you do.

Have you noticed that people who are at ease and relaxed often don't take themselves too seriously and can tolerate the ridiculous? It's hard to sustain feeling distressed while laughing! Let us look at cartoons, clowning, slapstick and situation comedy; they all make fun of the human condition. We identify with the subjects, get in touch with the absurdity in life, laugh, and diffuse our anger or distress.

A woman I know, who enjoys drawing, has introduced a playful approach into her frustrating experiences by designing cartoons. After sketching herself red faced and shaking with rage she finds that having expressed her anger she is ready to deal with the situation calmly. Occasionally, she produces a second drawing in which she makes the changes that would move her towards feeling more contented. She solves the problems on paper before getting down to brass tacks.

Change the language

You might do yourself a good service if you could cut out of your vocabulary words like 'ought', 'must' and 'should'. These are all words that place you firmly in the passive role of someone who does not make your own decisions. You might find that you are much more comfortable with 'prefer', 'choose', 'wish', 'want', 'decide'. You might even decide to do something you find unpleasant but the decision places you firmly at the helm, and you will tolerate the discomfort because it is your choice.

> Try changing the following sentences to an assertive alternative:
> I must dig the garden this weekend.
> I ought not to eat that cream cake.
> I should be studying but I can't concentrate.
> I've got to visit my invalid aunt today.
>
> Now make up a few examples of your own.

Let go of the pain

Some people find that their lives are much enriched if they allow themselves to have experiences in the here and now without expectations of the future or regrets for the past. They free themselves of wasted energy that so many of us expend on painful memories. They have no room for the 'if only' form of thinking.

Some years ago I visited a resettlement group home where I met James, a man in his seventies. He had spent much of his life in hospitals and now faced, for the rest of his life, this shared accommodation including his small bedsit, where he was surrounded by his own books and pictures. In this room, a budgie flew in and out of its cage, resting occasionally on my companion's hand. He explained that this bird exemplified what he called his 'open hand approach to life'. He told me that whatever alighted on his hand (or in his life) he would experience without grabbing it. His hand stayed open so that, when the experience went, he would not try to hold on to it. What he was describing was a life without expectation and, therefore, no disappointment. Each experience was lived, either with pain or pleasure but without attachment or resistance to it.

I am not suggesting that you should blot the past from your life. If you want to learn from experiences, it is necessary to remember them. What I do suggest is that you try to let go of the pain of past hurts. You have the choice of going over and over things that cause distress, of punishing yourself again and again. You might brood and say 'I shall remember how awful it was until my dying day' or you could say 'That was a bad experience, now I can let go of the pain and get on with my life.'

Recognize your rights

If you have duties, then also, you have rights. These are not concessions given to you by others but are to do with what you feel is basic to you. (Remember, what you do not have is the right to violate the needs of others.)

Here are some of the personal rights that have been suggested to me by members of my groups.

You have the right:

to be treated with respect	to laugh
to succeed	to cry
to express your feelings/opinions	to fail
not to assert yourself if you so choose	to do nothing
to have privacy	to change
to give yourself time	to give yourself space

You may not consider all of these to be important. Add to the list anything that is meaningful to you.

COMBATING ACTIVE DISTRESS

Do you, from time to time, get caught up in *active distress*? Do you feel that your wires are overloaded and that you might easily 'blow a fuse'? Perhaps you find yourself caught up in unproductive behaviour: losing your temper, grumbling, spending a lot of time on a task but achieving little. Or you might be distressed because you are altering your pattern of eating, drinking, smoking. Sometimes others recognize these symptoms before you do. Trust the observations of people you respect. You may be way above your Comfortable Functioning Level (*see* chapter 3). On the other hand, you may be happy with a lot of creative stress but find that what you are experiencing is the wrong type of pressure; that you are in a state of alert that taxes you but gives you no sense of achievement. Once the alarm bells ring, you are ready to STOP and STAND BACK.

Some of the following suggestions might help you. If you start to feel that they are a tyranny, you will be adding to your distress. It is for you to choose those ideas that will be a genuine aid.

Make a thought chart

Your thoughts could well be chasing themselves round your mind. Attempting to get yourself organized just makes you feel more tense. Try writing down any thoughts that occur to you; just random words will do. Don't put them in any order, but let them fall haphazardly on to the page. After a while you may find yourself able to link ideas, move them into some order, decide what is relevant and what is not.

When I want to plan a new course of lessons I find the

thought chart most helpful. I write down any topics that could possibly be included, I just let them tumble straight out of my mind on to the paper. Sometimes I write them on small, separate pieces of paper, then I start to move them about, deciding what is essential and what could be left out if I ran out of time. Some items are really part of the same topic and can be connected and I start to see where I need to begin and the order evolves.

Review the situation

This is where you make a list, either mentally or in writing. You are then in a position to develop an overview. You can determine priorities and decide what is essential and non-essential.

Make a list of important areas in your life at the moment.
Note those over which you have no control.
Those that you can control can be divided into ones which can be:

    a) dropped altogether
    b) postponed
    c) delegated
    d) dealt with immediately

Separate:

    1 the time needed to think or plan
    2 the time needed to carry out the task

Overloaded times

There are always some times when you have to make choices in your activities. If you have reached saturation point you may have to change 'I can't take it on' to 'I can't take it on in addition to everything else.' This may lead you to reassess your priorities. It is often possible to anticipate times when you are likely to get over-loaded, which is when you might find yourself saying 'I can't take that on at present.'

I used to find the first month of the teaching year very demanding. There were new children to get to know, new courses, much administration, many meetings . . . so September was not a month for me to have house guests, parties, or anything likely to put extra strain on me. This was the time to protect myself by cutting down on any extraneous activity, however pleasurable. The parties and outings had to be postponed until I had the energy to enjoy them.

Learn from experience

There are usually patterns in the periods of congestion and you would do well to anticipate them. Think of the build-up before and after holidays, at Christmas or when moving premises. If possible, you should plan ahead to protect yourself from burn-out, rather than wait for the distress signals. A good way to do this is to think back to a pre-vious similar occasion. Assess whether or not you dealt with it successfully, decide what could be repeated or what needs to be changed. Did you choose the correct priorities? Is there anything that could have been eliminated or that should have been added? From past experience, what would indicate to you that you need to stop and think again.

Pace yourself

You know your capacity and it is your duty to yourself to stay within it. You need to set limits on your available time, capacity and personal choices. If you have set aside relaxing times, allow them to stay that way. You know your own way of working, whether you are happier with short sharp bursts or long hauls. You may find that you have to state this and be prepared to negotiate with others who may have very different patterns. Remember, there is no right or wrong. You need confidence in whatever works for you but it is necessary to respect the needs of those who function differently, and compromises sometimes have to be made. Some people find it helpful to state to themselves, or to others, comments such as:

It looks as if we have different priorities/values/ perspectives.
We probably have very different ways of dealing with that.

Timetable

Not everything can be done at once and it is amazingly freeing to be able to space out your commitments. If you are not able to do this, you may find yourself having to focus again and again on what you are not yet able to do in order to keep it fresh in your memory. This is energy wasting and unnecessarily stressful.

> Think of a particular activity that you want to do but know that it cannot be done immediately.
> Plan some future time when you will be free and decide to postpone all thought of the activity until then.
> Allocate the time and make a mental or actual note of your decision.
> You are now free of the tyranny of nagging guilt.

Once you are able to plan ahead you might find yourself making statements such as: 'Thank you for lending me that book. I'd like to read it on holiday in June. Do you want it back until then, or shall I hang on to it?' or 'I really want to dig over and replant that flower bed. I'm not going to have time, so I guess it won't happen this year. I'll review it again next spring.'

Delegate

If you are unable to delegate and accept the support of others you may need to ask yourself a few searching questions.

Do you need to justify your existence?
Do you need to be indispensable?
Do you find it difficult to trust the competence of others?

Once you discover that there is no virtue in doing it all yourself, you will find yourself facing risks: it may be done worse than if you did it yourself; it may be done better. The only certainty is that it will be done differently. Other people are not, and should not be, clones of yourself. If this is a problem for you, reconsider your expectations. By using delegation creatively you are moving from being an operator to being a facilitator, which is a separate skill worth developing.

Back-up help

A lawyer friend of mine has the reputation of having a phenomenal memory. I asked him for his secret. He assured me that there was no secret. He did not, in fact, carry all knowledge in his head. He was very economical of his brain space and made good use of the expertise of others; he knew how to access information, how to use references, how to use notes. It is not valuable to aim at having all the answers. 'I don't know' is a valid answer provided it is followed by 'but I will find out'.

Tame your internal imp

Teresa, a mature student, had allocated a week to work on a difficult essay. Every time she sat at her desk, she noticed some small household chore that just had to be done – the picture wasn't straight, there was a smudge on the mirror. By the end of the week she had cleaned out all her cupboards and packed her freezer with home-made cakes . . . The essay was never completed. Her imp had won!

The *procrastination trap* is a demonstration of the internal imp at its most destructive. You have to find ways of dealing with the temptation to focus on unimportant sidetracking. It may be necessary to allocate a later time to deal with the intrusive chore. You may need to say, 'I can see that the picture is not straight. I shall deal with it in an hour's time when I get up to make myself a cup of coffee.' 'My desk drawer needs sorting out, but not today. I shall spend 30 minutes on it on Thursday afternoon once this report is complete.' You may find, to your surprise, that once the allotted time comes round, you have no interest in doing the chore. Your internal imp, once thwarted, has decided to leave you alone.

Use coping statements

In chapter 9 I dealt with the use of key words and affirmations. If this is a valuable aid for you, then this is the time to prepare suitable statements either to spur yourself on or to help you stay cool. If you are a very harsh self-critic, you may want to start by reminding yourself that nobody's perfect.

There are two questions that you might like to ask yourself:

1 **Whose problem is this?**
   It is very easy to get caught up in a tangle in which you could be taking on board a problem that belongs to someone else (eg I'm worried because my son is worried that I'm worried about him!). There is a big difference between solving your own problems and giving aid to others who are in trouble. When you help others you are offering the strength of your support which is all the

more effective because you are not focusing on your own emotional involvement.

2 **What is the worst that can happen?**
It is easy to lose perspective when in a panic. Facing up to the possible outcome could help you analyse the situation which could pave the way to coping. Once you think it through, you may even find that it is not half as bad as you first felt.

COMBATING PASSIVE DISTRESS

You readily recognize when 'things get too much' for you but do you sometimes find that 'things get too little'? Being underwhelmed can cause distress which could result in poor self-esteem, depression or just a feeling that life is passing you by.

People who function below their Comfortable Stress Level suffer from boredom. They sense that matters crucial to their welfare are slipping beyond their control. They need active participation and responsibility to put them in touch with their world, and restore their sense of purpose and well-being.

Understimulation sometimes moves in a downward spiral. Once people are doing little, they soon find that they do even less. The activities left for a holiday period, if boredom is present, often never get done. There is a saying that if you want something done, ask a busy person.

When people are engaged in non-demanding, repetitive jobs, they are more likely to have accidents because they are not sufficiently stimulated to pay attention. They are also more likely to end up over-tired and less satisfied. Robot people (and there is a robot in everyone) are also likely, through habituation, to have a programmed 'mind set' which makes it difficult for them to see the world through fresh eyes. For example, a notice in a works canteen read 'Happy Chrismas'. None of the regulars saw the error.

Similarly, if you show a group of people a piece of paper with 'Paris in the the Spring' written on it, most of them will read what they are used to seeing.

Redress the balance

Some people find the need to redress the balance of understimulating work with exciting hobbies or sporting activities. Sometimes this is done vicariously by getting involved in spectator sports or reading or watching pulse-quickening adventures. Some people with very sedate lives have the most hair-raising dreams.

You may want to make some concrete plans to bring more creative stress into your life.

Ring the changes

Changes may need to be made in your daily pattern. You could think of how to break with routine or bring an element of surprise into your day.

On one of those dreary English summer days, many years ago, when the rain drizzled constantly and my children hit a low and wailed, 'There's nothing to do!' I said, in a moment of inspiration, 'Yes there is, we'll have some lunch – but not at the table, under it!' Suddenly they were propelled into action – preparing the food, setting out plates on the floor, throwing a bedsheet over the table to make a tent. I was eventually invited to crawl in and join in the giggling at the jolly party.

It is worth giving some thought to how an 'under-the-table' approach can be introduced to a working day, a weekend, sexual relations or leisure pursuits.

Learn from the past

If life was rosy in the past but has now become dreary, you could think of what could be reintroduced into your routine. You might find yourself thinking something like, 'I always did intend to take up painting again when I had more time.' *or* 'I loved dancing when I was young. Perhaps I could have a go now.'

Your internal imp might jump in again at this point and cause you to focus on what has been lost and can never be retrieved. You need to remind yourself to be realistic. If you have sustained a loss – of a companion, your vigour, your income – making plans that are impossible leaves you bereft and in more pain. You may need to give extra thought to how to comfort yourself and then try to enrich your life in ways that are suitable to your current situation.

Move towards success

> Give your current position a grade on a scale of 1 to 10.
> What would have to happen to bring your score up two or three points?
> What would you have to do to make these things happen?

When people are feeling down they tend to push away offers of help and support. Once you are open to change there is much that is available

Environmental support – people

close family and friends   neighbours   colleagues
health professionals   psychotherapist/counsellor
religious leader

Environmental support – places

adult college courses   career advice
voluntary work   self-help groups
the arts (music, art, theatre)   sport

Things to do alone

listen to music   read
play an instrument   write letters/make phone calls
draw/paint/model   sew, knit, crochet

gardening
decorating
walk/hike/run
crosswords/jigsaw puzzles
plan a holiday

cooking
photography
sort out a cupboard/drawer
learn a new skill/language

Have a list of things that you want to get done some time. Refer to it when you can't make a decision. Try to do something new each week or each month.

Life is too precious to waste. Do things now!

SAYING 'NO' WITHOUT GUILT

If this is a difficult area for you, check out the following questions:

Do you get any satisfaction from being a martyr?
Do you feel that you must always do as others request?
Are you afraid that you will be disliked?
Are you prepared to risk the disapproval of others?

The first thing you will have to accept is that, as an imperfect human being, you are bound to let people down sometimes. You may have to be prepared to survive their hurt and say, 'I'm sorry I have to disappoint you.'

Recognize the manipulative ploys that some people use:

'I'm in terrible trouble . . .' (appealing to you, the rescuer).
'I know how kind/dependable you are . . .' (appealing to you to live up your reputation).
'I know I can rely on you . . .' (appealing to you to live up to *their* opinion of you).

Watch it! You're being set up!

You have the right not to attempt to measure up to the expectations of others. You might have to refute their statement, 'I'm afraid I'm not always able to be kind/dependable/clever. I'm afraid I can't be relied upon this time.' Even though you are about to say no, you want to show concern for the dilemma of the other people, so show that you understand their problem rather than giving a list of excuses that means you end up talking about yourself. Don't compete by relating your problems or say things like 'I'm a rotten friend' that will turn the focus on to you. A rejection of a request might go something like this:

1 State supportively that you understand the problem.
2 Say 'no'.
3 a) Offer what you could do.
  b) Suggest alternatives.

Here is an example:

1 You would like me to help you to repair that chair.
2 I'm sorry to disappoint you. I just haven't the time at present.
3 a) I could do it for you in a few months when I've dealt with my backlog.
  b) If you don't want to wait, I could give you the name of someone who might be able to do it for you.

Here are a few extreme requests. Try saying 'no' without losing a friendship.

---

1 I'm going away for four weeks. Would you please come in every day to look over the house, water the plants, feed the fish and cut the grass once a week? I know I can rely on you!
2 You are such a kind person. I'm having a meeting here next week for 40 people. Would you and your partner come to make the coffee?
3 I'm in terrible trouble! I know you're in the middle of a dinner party, but I have to meet Madeline at the airport and my car won't start. Can you drive me?

GOING FORWARD WITH ACTION PLANS

If you want to make important changes or develop new schemes for yourself, you will need to make certain that success is built into your programme. You should establish a pathway that takes you, undaunted, towards your target. A small amount of time spent planning makes a good investment.

State your current situation

Once you state, specifically, your current situation, you have started to analyse what is worth preserving and what needs to change. This will help you determine your aim, and will give you a base from which to assess progress. If you don't know where you are coming from, you cannot judge how far you've moved.

State your aim – the major objective

Check out that you are being *realistic*. Control your internal imp and avoid indulging in an element of fantasy that has failure built into the plan. Be careful not to aim at something that could reinforce a sense of low self-esteem so that the imp says, 'There, I always knew you couldn't do it!'

> Penelope had a fairly good voice. She dreamed of becoming a great singer, but, now in her mid thirties, she had not yet given a recital. She developed a chronic throat spasm which she blamed for her lack of professional progress. After much soul searching, she changed her aim and decided to be more realistic in her expectations. Her throat spasm relaxed and she settled into enjoying semi-professional engagements which suited her ability.

Keep your aim *positive*. State where you are going rather than focus on what you want to leave behind. So instead of 'I wish I were not such a misery' you would say 'I would really like to allow some fun into my life.'

Develop the aim and make it *specific*. 'I wish I were better organized,' is vague and doesn't point at a direction. Try instead, 'I should like to keep my desk tidy, file papers more carefully and keep to a better schedule.' By being specific you are analysing the situation and gaining an insight into a possible solution.

Acknowledge risks

You are embarking on an adventure which will be scary as well as exciting. Remaining static, however uncomfortable, is at least predictable. There is a saying that the devil you know is better than the devil you have yet to meet. (If you feel like this, you may prefer to give up.) It is as well to know what the risks are. Perhaps it is difficult to let go of a long-held view of yourself or a view others have held of you. You have a right to change, but remember that others may have to change along with you. Family dimensions or work relationships may alter. You may need to review your progress and make adjustments to your plan and even decide that you made a poor choice. Allowing adaptability into your programme makes you vulnerable. Can you cope? Do you have the courage?

Minor objectives

Make a list of easily attainable steps rather than large leaps forward. You might like to create a *thought chart* to help you establish criteria. You are looking for small successes that will pull you along in your progress. Minor objectives cannot be too small and insignificant. The more you can establish achievement, the better will be your motivation.

Review

Think over why you were successful and how you can improve on aspects which were not so good. Try to be specific rather than say 'that was good or bad'. Analysis help you to learn from the experience.

Rewards

Give yourself plenty of positive encouragement. Recording progress, crossing items off a list, or giving yourself a word of praise or a small reward all act as reinforcements. Some people like to take a break after each small task.

Don't forget to celebrate when the major objective is achieved.

Tear up a number of pieces of paper.
On one side write a significant area of your life (eg family, leisure, work, health).
On the other side, write some small change in an area that would enhance your life.
Design a pathway of minor objectives that could help you to achieve that aim.

GIVE YOURSELF TREATS AND HAVE FUN

You know that having a good time is good for your physical and psychological well-being. Pleasure and spontaneity are the keys to self-expression. They are your right and need not be deserved. People love and care for their children, give them lots of fun and a good time and want to encourage them to make life a good experience. They are generally less generous with the 'child within'. But this is the part of a person that grows, changes and is creative. It needs nurturing.

Let me remind you that when things are getting heavy you should:

Stop – Step back – Have fun!

I still carry with me the cherished memory of a dear woman who was my teacher when I was nine years old. On the last day in her class, when we were facing the long summer holiday, she presented each of us with a notebook. She asked us to write down, each day, something that was beautiful or wonderful. Her brand of education could not be assessed in standardized tests!

Treats need not be expensive and do not have to be concrete. Rewarding yourself with fattening food as you reach a minor objective on a slimming programme might be counter-productive. Planning a world-wide trip that you know you will never afford, just because you think you deserve it, will only lead to disappointment. You will do yourself a favour if you are realistic both about your lifestyle and about what you really like, rather than what you think you ought to like. This also applies if you want to treat others. It is not much use making a surprise party for someone who enjoys a quiet dinner for two, or a weekend in a country retreat for a townie.

Make a list of treats for yourself:

1 that cost nothing.
2 that cost a small enough amount not to cause financial hardship.

In which situations might you give yourself these treats?

Don't wait for other people to give you a good time. Go for it! Life itself is the most precious gift of all. Be open to all it has to offer. I end with an old Maori saying:

Turn your face to the sun and the shadows fall behind you.

Further Reading

Bieber, J, *If Divorce is the Only Way*, Penguin Books Ltd, 1997

Breton, S, *Depression*, Element Books, 1996

Brennan, R, *Alexander Technique*, Element Books, 1997

Fast, J, *Body Language*, Pan Books, 1980

Field, L, *Self-Esteem for Women*, Element Books, 1997

Fontana, D, *Know Who You Are. Be What You Want*,
    Element Books, 1997

Harrison, K, *Vitamins & Minerals in a Nutshell*, Element Books,
    1997

Help – a practical guide to life's ups and downs, HMSO, 1996

Markham, U, *Bereavement*, Element Books, 1996

Rowe, D, *Dorothy Rowe's Guide to Life*, HarperCollins, 1995

Sutherland, S, *Irrationality – The Enemy Within*, Constable, 1992

Wildwood, C, *Aromatherapy*, Element Books, 1991

Woodall, M K, *How to Think on Your Feet*, Thorson
    Business Series,

Useful Addresses

General

Local Adult Education Colleges: look for classes in Assertiveness, Stress Management, Keep Fit.

Local Health Promotion Unit courses in good health practice: Nutrition, Exercise, Quitting Smoking.

Details in telephone book or local library.

Counselling and Psychotherapy

United Kingdom

National Council of Psychotherapists
Hazelwood
Broadmead
Sway
Lymington
Hants SO41 6DH
Tel: 01590 683770

British Association for Counselling
1 Regent Place
Rugby
Warwickshire CV21 2PJ
Tel: 01788 578328

Cruse
Cruse House
126 Sheen Road
Surrey TW91 1UR
(bereavement counselling)

Eire

Irish Association for Counselling
11 Rock Hill
Main Street
Blackrock
Co. Dublin

USA

International Association of Counselors and Therapists
8313 West Hillsborough Avenue
Suite 480
Tampa
Florida 33615
Tel: 813 877 5592

American Association for
Counseling &
International Association of
Counseling Services
5999 Stevenson Avenue
Alexandria
VA 22304
Tel: 703 823 9840

Canada

Canadian Guidance &
Counseling Association
00-22- Lauria Avenue West
Ottawa
Ontario K1P 5
Tel: 613 2230 4236

The Centre of International
Holistic Studies
298 Grays Road
Unit 6
Hamilton
Ontario L8E 1V5
Tel: 905 6622 7463

Australia

Australian Psychological
Society
National Science Centre
191 Royal Parade
Victoria 5075

New Zealand

New Zealand Association of
Counsellors
17 Corokia Place
Manukau City
Auckland
Tel: 09 267 5973

Belgium (French and Flemish)

Info Geesstelijke
Gezondheidszorg
Bosstraat 12
TE 1050
Brussels
Tel: 26 49 56 65

France

Union Internationale des
Organismes Familiaux
28 Place Saint-George
75009 Paris
Tel: 48 78 0759

Germany

Gestalt Education Network
International (GENI)
Oberweg 54
D60000 Frankfurt
Tel: 69 55 98 67

Netherlands

Nederlandse Verenigen van
Opvoedkuudigen
Onderwijskundigen en
Andrologen
Korte Elisabethstraat 11
3511 Utrecht

Marriage & Relationship Guidance

United Kingdom

Relate
Herbert Gray College
Little Church Street
Rugby CV21 3AP
Tel: 01788 57 3241

National Association of
Family Mediation and
Conciliation Services
Shaftesbury Centre
Percy Street
Swindon
Wilts SN2 2AZ
(co-ordinating body for
independent out-of-court
services nationwide)

USA

American Association of
Marriage & Family Counselors
255 Yale Avenue
Claremont
California

Australia

Australian Association of
Marriage & Family
Counsellors
12 Payton Avenue
Dernancourt
S A 5075

Hypnotherapy

United Kingdom

National Council for
Hypnotherapy
Hazelwood
Broadmead
Sway
Lymington
Hants SO41 6DH
Tel: 01590 683770

USA

American Board of
Hypnotherapy
16842 Von Carmen Avenue
Suite 475
Irvine
California 92714
Tel: 714 261 6400

Australia

Australian Hypnotherapy
Association
15 Chauvel Avenue
Milperra
NSW 2214

Yoga & Transcendental Meditation

United Kingdom

British Wheel of Yoga
1 Hamilton Place
Boston Road
Sleaford
Lincs NG34 7 ES
Tel: 015129 306 851

Yoga Fellowship of Northern
Ireland
16 Kinghill Road
Rathfriland
Co Down BT34 5RB
Tel: 018206 31138

Edinburgh & Lothian Yoga
Association
10 Buckstowe Way
Edinburgh EH10 6PW
Tel: 0131 445 2947

Freepost
London SW1P 4YY
National Enquiry Helpline:
0990 143733
(transcendental meditation)

Eire

An Sanctoir
Co. Cork
Tel: 284336

Australia

Self-Realisation Meditation
Healing Centre
53 Regent Street
Paddington
NSW 2021

New Zealand

Self-Realisation Meditation
Healing Centre
100 Highsted Road
Bishopdal
Christchurch
Tel: 3 359 8507

USA

Unity in Yoga International
PO Box 281004
Lakewood
Colorado 80228

Drinkline

United Kingdom

National Alcoholic Helpline:
Tel: 0345 320202

Samaritans (telephone help for the despairing)

United Kingdom

National Number:
Tel: 0345 909090

Northern Ireland

Belfast. Tel: 1232 664 422

Eire

Dublin. Tel: 1 872 7700
Cork. Tel: 21 271323

USA

Washington DC.
Tel: 202 362 8100
Boston. Tel: 617 247 0220
New York. Tel: 212 673 3000

Canada

S Alberta. Tel: 403 320 1212

Australia

Springwood NSW.
Tel: 47 51 6402
Perth WA. Tel: 93 81 5555

New Zealand

Wellington. Tel: 4 473 9739-40
Christchurch. Tel: 3 366 6676

Lone Parents and Children

United Kingdom

Gingerbread Association for
one-parent families
16 Clerkenwell Close
London EC1
Tel: 0171 336 8184

Gingerbread Northern Ireland
Tel: 01232 231 414

Gingerbread Scotland
Tel: 0141 353 0953

Aromatherapy

United Kingdom

Aromatherapy Organisations
Council
3 Latymer Close
Braybrooke
Market Harborough
Leicester LE16 8LN
Tel: 01858 434242

Products:
Dept 2, Verde
15 Flask Walk
Hampstead
London NW3
Tel: 0870 603 9186

Index

Details of Cassette

Rochelle Simmons can be heard on cassette on which she talks you through a relaxation session (side A) and provides a visualization for relaxation (side B).

Send a cheque to:

Rochelle Simmons
PO Box 17411
London NW7 3ZD

Prices (including postage and packing)
(*sterling only*)

UK	£7–95
Republic of Ireland	£8–40
Canada, South Africa, USA	£8–90
Australia, New Zealand	£9–10